THE
KAYANS

THE
KAYANS

A Journey through their
Rich Cultural Heritage and Legacy

Richard Ibuh

PARTRIDGE
A Penguin Random House Company

To order additional copies of this book, contact
Toll Free 800 101 2657 (Singapore)
Toll Free 1 800 81 7340 (Malaysia)
orders.singapore@partridgepublishing.com

www.partridgepublishing.com/singapore

Contents

1

The Kayan Tribe

Kayan as we readily have known is the name of a tribe found in Borneo. The Kayan people are categorized as part of the *Dayak* communities of Borneo. How the word '*Dayak*' came about is uncertain. Some think that it is derived from the Brunei Malay word '*daya*' which means '*inland*' or '*interior*'. Nevertheless, Gomes (1911) is of the view that '*the derivation is quite incorrect to apply it to all the inland races of Borneo - there are many tribes such as the Kayans, Muruts, Ukits, and Punans, who are not Dayaks at all, their language, customs, and traditions being quite different*'.

Being an indigenous tribe in central Borneo, the Kayans are similar to their neighbours the Kenyah tribe with which they are grouped together under the *Bahau* ethnic group. The population of the Kayan group in 2010 is in the region of 30,000 or about 1.2% of Sarawak population. They are part of the larger grouping of people referred to collectively as the *Orang Ulu* - 'upriver people'. The Kayans like the other *Dayak* tribes in those earlier times were known for being fierce warriors, head-hunters, adept in hill-paddy cultivation, and having extensive and elaborate tattoos and stretched earlobes amongst both the men and women. Older women usually have pierced earlobes, stretched distinctively through wearing heavy metal earrings.

The *Orang Ulu* "peoples of the interior" is a name used by most of the native Dayak ethnic groups of Sarawak to describe, identify and differentiate them. Numerically the Dayaks are the largest grouping in Sarawak in 2010, accounting for 1,068,300 or 43.2% of the population. Other ethnic groups are Malays (22.9%), Melanau (4.9%) and Chinese (23.4%). The other Bumiputras of Sarawak which comprises the *Orang Ulu* were 156,436, that accounted for about 6.3% of the overall population. The Dayaks are a diverse group, with many different tribes and sub-tribes, and are part of the much larger Dayak community of the island of Borneo, three-quarters of which is the Indonesian provinces of Kalimantan. The total population of Sarawak in 2010 was 2,471,140 (State Planning Unit, 2011).

The Kayans of Sarawak were postulated to have originated from along the Kayan River in Kalimantan Borneo. They have lived along the upper Kayan and the middle Kapuas and Mahakam rivers. It was pointed that the Kayans may have expanded to the south in Sarawak in earlier times, thus generating conflicts with the Ibans that were expanding north at the same time. Due to those incessant fights, the Kayans were pushed inland whereby they migrated northwards where they finally settled along the middle Baram River, upper Kemena River and the upper Rajang River, where they are still generally found today.

The Kayan language belongs to the Malayo-Polynesian branch of the Austronesian language. Nonetheless, like all other indigenous tribes of Borneo, the Kayans have no alphabet, mode of writing or knowledge of letters, nor do they practice any systematically drawn method of representing their ideas by figures. With the exception of local differences, all the sub-groups of the tribe speak the same language so as to be understood by each other throughout their wide distribution of settlements. The Kayan language though is copious, pleasantly soft and comparatively easy to learn. Their language differs entirely from that of the Ibans and Bidayuhs. Their basic culture is nonetheless, similar to the other Dayaks of Borneo.

Traditionally they live in longhouses along the river banks that have been their main means of communication and livelihood. In the past, their main agriculture activity is the cultivation of hill-paddy planting based on the shifting cultivation or *swidden* farming. They also cultivated sago, tapioca, fruits, went hunting and fishing. The Kayans are known for their good wood carvings and metal works.

As highlighted by Roth (1968), Sir James Brooke described the Kayans as follows:

> *'In stature they are of moderate height, but stout limb and fleshy. Their complexion is fairer than any of the other tribes; their faces round, fat, and good tempered; eyes small and well formed; and mouth expressive; and altogether with very few characteristics of the Malays, certainly much better looking men - as well as strong or wiry-looking men, capable of much fatigue'. 'As for the women, they are tolerable looking with pleasant countenances. Their countenances were open, bright dark eyes, smooth foreheads, depressed noses, clear skin, but indifferent mouths. They had good figures and well set up busts, the young girls have regular features, light skins, and good figures, with a pleasing pensive expression.*

The Kayans are especially lithe and active - bronzy, straight-limb and statuesque. This the result of an active life spent hunting in the forest, climbing after gutta, rubber, jungle-fruits, or bees honey, or in cultivating the clearings around their dwellings, or in fishing in the rivers.' Nonetheless, how do we see the Kayan Uma Pu women from the picture shown here, compared to those in Burma and how James Brooke saw them?

A big part of the Kayan group in Baram though moved inland from Batu Talang to Long *Nahah'A* for one group, with a big part of the group moving into Patah River and finally the majority of them pushing further down to the Apoh river valley and settled at Long Belanah. The remaining group in Patah finally move over to Long Bemang. A portion of the remaining group in Batu Talang finally migrated to Long Bemang in the 1930s - rowing and flowing down the main Baram River.

They were received at Apoh River mouth and escorted up the Apoh River to Long Bemang by the Long Atip-Long Bedian group, who are instrumental in urging them to migrate to Apoh River valley.

The Kayans in the Apoh River valley are found in the villages of Long Bemang, Long Atip, Long Bedian and Long Wat. The Kayans of Sungai Apoh villages of Long Bemang, Long Atip and Long Bedian, are from the **Uma Pu** group. In Long Wat though, about 30 doors of the village are from the Kenyah ethnic group. They were the original settlers of the village. The Kayan community of Long Wat originally came from Patah River and they are also from the **Uma Pu** group.

Elongated ear is the pride and culture of Kayan maidens in the older generations

Thus, the enduring survival and existence of the Kayans has been due their cohesiveness and cooperative nature. As Hose (1926; 1988) emphasized, the way the Kayans hang together and keep in touch with one another, even though scattered through districts in which numerous communities of other tribes are settled, preserving their characteristic culture with extreme faithfulness, lends credibility to the supposition that that the whole tribe may thus have been displaced step by step, passing from one region and from one island to another without leaving behind any part of the tribe. The parts of their tribal migration that are most difficult to comprehend are the passage of the straits between the Peninsula and Sumatra, and between Sumatra and Borneo. We do know though, that Kayans do not fear to put to sea in their long war boats, and follow the coast round the island and for considerable distances.

One piece of history that is never ever to be repeated by the modern Kayans is as written by Gomes (1911) as follows:

> *"The Kayans and Kinyehs, who may be classed together, are a numerous race inhibiting the upper waters of the Baram and Rejang Rivers. In many ways they seem to be a more advanced race than the Sea Dyaks. They build better houses, and are more expert in the manufacture of weapons, being able to extract their iron from the native ore. Their moral character, however, is vindictive and cruel, and they are lacking in that spirit of hospitality which is a great feature of the Sea Dyak character. A few years ago a party of Dyak gutta-percha collectors were attacked by the Punans, and many of them killed. Four young Dyaks managed to escape, and after wandering for many days in the jungle, arrived destitute and starving at a Kayan house, and asked for food and shelter. The treatment they received was horrible in the extreme. The Kayans bound the young men, and after breaking their arms and legs, handed them over to the women, who slowly despatched them by hacking them to pieces with little knives"*
>
> Gomes, (1911) p. 34

This incident should serve as a lesson for all the indigenous tribes of Borneo to hold steadfastly to the spirit of brotherhood, especially in this modern era. The lack of understanding like in the past should never ever happen again amongst the *Dayaks* and with the Kayans and *Orang Ulus* of Sarawak in particular. By the love and grace of God we must forgive and forget our bad and terrible past.

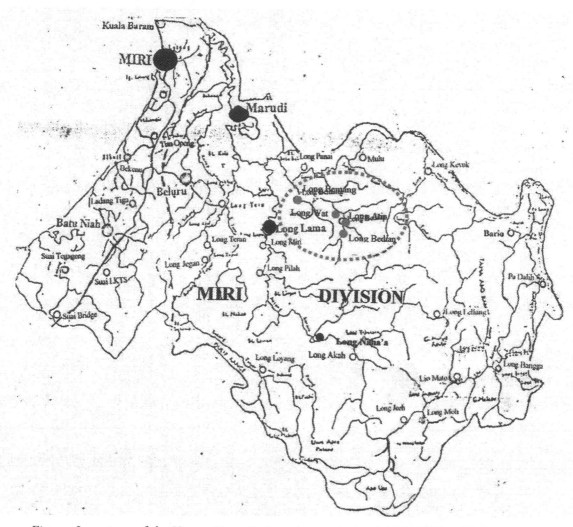

Figure: Locations of the Kayan ***Uma Pu*** Longhouses in Apoh River Valley. Drawn map

Hose (1926; 1988) pointed that, there can be little doubt that the **Kayans** of today are the descendants of emigrants from the mainland, and that they brought with them all or most of their characteristic culture. The Kayans migrated to Borneo from the basin of the Irrawaddy by way of Tenasserim, the Malay Peninsula, and Sumatra. They represent a part of the Indonesian stock which has remained in the basin of the Irrawaddy and adjacent rivers from the time of the separation of Borneo.

It looks like the **Kayans** are not confined to the Island of Borneo alone. There are the Kayans of the sub-group of the Red Karen (Karenni) people, a Tibeto-Burman ethnic minority of Myanmar or Burma. The Kayans in Burma consists of the following groups: Kayan Lahwi (also called

Padaung, Kayan Ka Khaung (Gekho), Kayan Lahta, Kayan Ka Ngan. Kayan Gebar, Kayan Kakhi, and sometimes called Kayaw. Padaung (Yan Pa Doung) is a Shan term for the Kayan Lahwi - the group whose women wear the brass neck coils. The Kayan residents in Mae Hong Son Province in Northern Thailand refer to themselves as Kayan. Women of the various Kayan tribes identify themselves by their different form of dress. Women of the Kayan Lahwi tribe are well known for wearing neck rings, brass coils that are placed around the neck, appearing to lengthen it. The women wearing these coils are known as *giraffe women* to tourists. Girls first start to wear rings when they are around five years old. Over the years the coil is replaced by a longer one, and more turns are added. The weight of the brass pushes the collar bone down and compresses the rib cage. The neck itself is not lengthened; the appearance of a stretched neck is created by the deformation of the clavicle bone. Many ideas as to why the coils are worn have been suggested, often formed by foreign anthropologists, who have hypothesized that the rings protected women from becoming slaves by making them less attractive to other tribes. Contrastingly it has been theorized that the coils originate from the desire to look more attractive by exaggerating sexual dimorphism, as women have more slender necks than men. It has also been suggested that the coils give the women resemblance to a dragon, an important figure in Kayan folklore. Nonetheless, the question is whether these tribes are from the common stock of the Kayans of Borneo?

However, Hose (1926; 1988) is of the view that it is highly probable that all these, together with the Kayans of Borneo, are the surviving branches of a people which occupied a large area of southeastern Asia, more especially the basin of the Irrawaddy, for a considerable period before the first of the successful invasions which gave rise to the existing Burmese and Shan states, and represent the original Indonesian population, of which the *Klemantans* of Borneo are the purest type modified by later infusions of Mongol blood. Thus, more ethnological study needs to be done to verify and substantiate the authenticity of these claims and presumptions.

When we make a search on who are the Kayan people on the internet, the sources found are about the Kayan in Burma or Myanmar and not in Borneo. Thus, this creates an interesting enquiry about the extent of distribution of the Kayan tribe in the world, especially in the Asia region.

Modern Kayan Uma Pu ladies showing a mix of identity with their past

2

The Kayan Social System

The Kayans constitute a well-defined and homogeneous tribe or community. Although their villages are scattered over a wide area, the Kayan people everywhere speak the same language and follow the same customs, have the same traditions, beliefs, rites, and ceremonies. Such small differences as they present from place to place are hardly obvious. Communication between the widely separated branches of the Kayans is very slight and infrequent, yet all are bound together by a common sentiment for the tribal name, reputation, tradition, and customs. The headman keeps in mind and hand down from generation to generation the history of the migrations of the principal branches of the tribe, the names and genealogies of the principal headman, and important incidents affecting any one branch.

In the past, there are various sub-tribes of the Kayans live harmoniously in the '*Apau Kayan*' in Kalimantan Borneo. They are normally settled by the confluence of rivers that form the name of each Kayan sub-tribe. For instance, those Kayans that settled at Long Bawang called themselves Kayan Uma Bawang. Those that settled at Long Semuka are known as Kayan Uma Semuka. The Kayan group that settled at Long Pako' are known as Kayan Uma Pako'. Those Kayans that settled at Long Peliau are known as Kayan Uma Peliau. And those Kayans that settled at Long Pu became known as Kayan Uma Pu. The names of these Kayan sub-tribes are still kept and maintained that segregate their specific identity from each other, till this present day.

There are about twenty sub-tribes of Kayans that are recognized, each bearing a distinctive name. The word UMA, which appears in the names of each group, means village or settlement, and it seems probable that these twenty sub-tribes represent twenty or less original Kayan villages which at some remote period, before the tribe became so widely scattered, may have contained the whole Kayan population - in '*Apau Kayan*'. Presently the people of each sub-tribe occupy several villages, which in most cases are within the basin of one river. The *Kayan Uma Pu* for instance, is mostly found in the Apoh River valley. Some remnants of *Kayan Uma Pu* are found in Central Baram River and Lower Tinjar River. In the Baram district, the Kayan sub-tribes are*: Uma Pu; Uma Beluvuh; Uma Semuka'; Uma Pliau; Uma Pako', Uma Bawang and Uma Belun.* The other Kayan tribes are found in Belaga District, and in Tubau.

Table: Kayan Sub-Tribes

District	Sub-Tribes
BARAM	Uma Pu, Uma *Beluvuh; Uma Semuka'; Uma Pliau; Uma Pako', Uma Bawang and Uma Belun.*
BELAGA	Uma Lesong, Uma Balui Ukap, Uma Daro', Uma Juman, Uma Liko, Uma Nyaving, Uma Bawang, Uma Apan, Uma Kahei, and Uma Aging.
TUBAU	Uma Anyi, Uma Juman, Uma Gong

Source: Persatuan Kayan Sarawak record

In spite of the community's tribal sentiment, which leads Kayans always to take side with their kinsman, and prevents the occurrence of any serious quarrels between Kayan villages, there exist no formal bonds between the various sub-tribes and villages. Each village is absolutely independent of all others, save in so far as custom and tradition subscribes it, before undertaking any important affair, such as a removal of the village or a warlike expedition, the headman will seek the advice, and, if necessary, the co-operation of the headman of neighbouring Kayan villages. The people of neighbouring villages, especially the families of the headman, are also bound together by many ties of kinship - for intermarriage is frequent. In the Apoh River valley, all the headmen are somewhat related to each other, being descendants of the *Maren Uma* or *Hipun Uma* of the *Uma Pu* tribal clan.

A Kayan village almost invariably may consist of several longhouses. Each longhouse is ruled by a headman, and the headman is recognized as the authority or government representative of the village.

The minor and purely domestic affairs of each house are settled by the individual household-head, but all important matters of general interest are brought before the village or longhouse headman. In the former category though, includes all disputes as to ownership of domestic animals and plants, questions of compensation for injury or loss of borrowed boats, nets, or other articles, of marriage and divorce, and minor personal injuries, moral or physical in nature. The matters to be settled by the village headman sitting in council with the village committee council are those affecting the whole village such as the questions of war and peace and of removal, disputes between houses, and trials for murder or serious personal injuries. These were the roles of the *Maren Uma* in the earlier times and during the period of the Rajah Brooke and British Colonial rule.

The degree of authority of the headman and the nature and degree of the penalties imposed by them are prescribed in a general way by custom, though as regards the former much depends upon the personal qualities of each household, and as regards the latter much is left to his discretion. The punishments imposed are generally fines in the form of *Tawaks* or gongs, *Parangs* or swords, spears, or other articles of personal property or value. On the whole the headman plays the part of an arbitrator and mediator, awarding compensation to the injured party, rather than that of a judge. In the case of offences against the whole house, a fine is imposed; and the articles of the required value are placed under the charge of the headman, who holds them on behalf of the community, and uses them in the making of payments or presents in return for services rendered to the whole community.

The headman also is responsible for the proper observation of the omens and for the regulation of *'Lalih'* or taboos affecting the whole house; and he takes the leading part in social ceremonies and in most of the religious rites collectively performed by the village. He is regarded by other household-head as responsible for the behaviour of his people, and above all, in war in the old days, he is responsible for both strategy and tactics and the general conduct of operations.

For the maintenance of his authority and the enforcement of his commands the headman relies upon the force of public opinion or community consensus which, so long as he is capable and just, will always support him, and will bring severe moral pressure to bear upon any member of the household who hesitates to submit to community norms and requirements.

In return for his labours on behalf of the household or village the Kayan headman gains little or nothing in the form of material reward. He may receive a little voluntary assistance in the cultivation of his field; in travelling by boat he is accorded the place of honour and ease in the middle of the boat, and he is not expected to help in its propulsion. His principal rewards are the social recognition, and prominence accorded to him and the satisfaction found in the exercise of authority.

The office of headman is hereditary, but operated in the context of elective principle which is affected by a strong bias in favour of the most capable son of the late headman; so in practice a headman is generally succeeded by one of his sons. An elderly headman will sometimes voluntarily abdicate in favour of a son. If a headman dies, leaving no son of mature age, some elderly man of good standing and capacity will be elected to the headman-ship, generally by agreement arrived at by many informal discussions during the weeks following the death. If thereafter a son of the old headman showed himself a capable man as he grew up, he would be held to have a strong claim on the headman-ship at the next vacancy. If the new headman at his death left also a mature and capable son, there might be two claimants, each supported by a strong party; the issue of such a state of affairs would probably be the division of the house or village, by the departure of one claimant with his party to build a new village. In such a case the seceding party would carry away with them their share of the timbers of the old house, together with all their personal property. Nonetheless, this rarely occurs in the Kayan community that reflects on the closely knit kinsmanship and cohesiveness of the people.

Among both Kayans and Kenyahs three social strata are clearly distinguishable and are recognised by the people themselves in each village. The upper class is constituted by the family of the headman and his near relatives, his aunts and uncles, brothers, sisters, and cousins, and their children. These upper-class families are generally in better positions and circumstances than the others, thanks to the possession of property such as brass ware, valuable beads, caves in which the swift builds its edible nest, slaves, and a supply of all the other material possessions larger in quantity and superior in quality to those of the middle-class and lower-class families. The three class structures are: the *Maren Uma* or the high aristocrats, the *Hipui* or *Maren Uk* are the noble folk and *Panyin* are the commoners. In the olden days, the Kayan society was strictly divided into four distinct social classes: *Maren, Hipui, Panyin and Dipen. Dipen* or slaves are found during the tribal conflicts and headhunting days that are obtained as captured enemies which is not practised today.

The man of the upper class can generally be distinguished at a glance by his superior bearing and manners, by the neatness and cleanliness of his person, his more valuable weapons, and personal ornaments, as well as by greater regularity of features. The woman of the upper class also exhibits to the eye similar marks of her superior birth and breeding. The tattooing of her skin is more finely executed; greater care is taken with the elongation of the lobe of the ear, so that the social status of the woman is indicated by the length of the lobe. Her dress and person are cleaner, and generally better cared for, and her skin is fairer than that of other women, owing no doubt to her having been less exposed to the sun.

As (Fong, 2008) pointed, the Kayans, Kenyahs and Kelabits have very clearly defined social class system, and the village chief or headman is well-respected person. These leaders are hereditary, and they received very strict training for leadership since a very young age.

The middle part of the village is where the 'maren uma' stays

In the longhouse the arrangement of the compartments of each family is separated according to the social classes. The headman's room, which is usually about twice as wide as others, is usually in the middle of the house; and those of the other upper-class families, which also may be larger than the other rooms adjoin it on either side, while those at the two ends of the longhouses are for the lower class (Fong, 2008). The house of the *Maren Uma* or headman is more conspicuous by the extended and protruded front portion of the veranda of the '*amin*' or '*bilik*'. And it is not allowed and very improper for other social classes of the longhouse folks to build similar extension to their '*amin*'. The extended veranda has its numerous purposes such as a meeting venue; community celebrations; community feasts; and other community functions for the village.

3

The great leaders of Kayan Uma Pu
and of the Apoh River Valley

According to folklores and oral tradition, there is a long line of generations of Kayan Uma Pu leaders. Available records and as deliberated at length by Ajeng (2004) are as follows:

'In the early times of the Kayan Uma Pu clan, the first five prominent individuals or 'Maren Uma' that led the Kayan Uma Pu are namely: Jok To; Emang Megen; Uyau La'ui; Item Ukun; and Jau Damuh. *Nonetheless, the pattern of leadership sequence is not certain, such as, who is the first leader and subsequent leaders are sketchy due to unclear oral folklores and lack of available documents.*

Nonetheless, when the Kayan group settled at Long Pu along the Batang Kayan River, the leadership or 'Maren Uma' became clearer. The leader of the Kayan Uma Pu then is Wan Jau. He is instrumental in leading the Kayan Uma Pu to migrate to 'Apau Bato' Liang Hagah' and the 'Leken Valley', where he died. His son Jau Wan took over as 'Maren Uma' until his death at 'Apau Bato' Liang Hagah'.

The next leader of the Kayan Uma Pu is Anyie Jau @ Jelivan, the son of Jau Wan. Jelivan was the man who brought his people to migrate from Kalimantan Borneo to Sarawak. Their migration journey is as follows: from Apau Bato' Liang Hagah to Lakuh valley in Linau; to Danum; and then moving onward to Pa'ung in upper reaches of the Tinjar; from there they move upward to Selaan River; and finally moving downward to settle at Long Nahah A or Batu Talang, where he died. Jelivan which is King Cobra is indeed akin to his name that is seen as fearless, courageous and powerful that instil a sense of trust, hope and loyalty of his followers. As such, he was able to lead his people on their migration without any resistance and in the process pushing aside the other tribes along their migration path.

After the demise of Anyie Jau @ Jelivan, his son Ngau Anyie @ Nyepa' took over as 'Maren Uma'. During his tenure of leadership however, the Kayan Uma Pu got divided and moved to three places around Batu Talang namely: Datah Tawak; Long Nyevung; and Long Benyu. Nonetheless, Nyepa as 'Maren Uma' is still the overall Chieftain of the Kayan Uma Pu. The main reasons for the division of the Kayan Uma Pu then are because the area around Batu Talang is hilly and unsuitable for farming. Furthermore, the group has become too large for the settlement.

Wan Ngau @ Taman Usung took over the Kayan Uma Pu leadership or Penghulu at the time of the emergence of the Rajah Brooke rule, which is around 1883 when the Sultan of Brunei ceded the Baram to Rajah James Brooke. Wan Ngau is the son of Ngau Anyie @ Nyepa. Thus, he is the rightful 'Maren Uma', although he is being challenged for the leadership by another man called Lake' Lah. However, the Brooke government was prudent and firm in awarding the Penghuluship to Wan Ngau. *Wan Ngau @ Taman Usung was instrumental in bringing the Long Atip – Long Bedian Kayan Uma Pu group to migrate to Apoh River valley in the early 1900s. He died at the time the group is settled at Long Belanah.*

The Brooke government readily appointed Jok Ngau @ Baya' as Penghulu after the demise of Wan Ngau @ Taman Usung that are brothers. Penghulu Baya' was entrusted as the Penghulu Kayan Uma Pu for Telang Usan and Apoh River. It was during his time as Penghulu that the Kayan Uma Pu migrated to two places namely: Long Pawan and Long Kelimau. During the migration to Long Pawan though, a portion of the group led by Anyi Lah and his brother instead went and settled at Datah Kelawit.

The next Penghulu after the death of Penghulu Jok Ngau @ Baya was Nyepa' Wan, his brother-in law. Penghulu Nyepa Wan was known to a man of fine character and good leadership acumen. *Unfortunately, his tenure as Penghulu was quite short.*

The new Penghulu appointed for the Kayan Uma Pu is Tama Paya Anyie @ Jelivan. Penghulu Tama Paya Anyie was also a 'dayong' or shaman. As such, he was held in high esteem and possessed mystical and magical powers that befits his name Jelivan or King Cobra. However, after he led the Kayan Uma Pu to embrace Christianity, he totally discarded the name Jelivan from his identity and record. Tama Paya Anyie was appointed Penghulu on 22nd March 1946 and retired on 30th June 1974. *His tenure as Penghulu of the Kayans was very significant because his leadership commenced at the time of the British Colonial rule right into the period of the formation of Malaysia.*

Ajeng, H.A., (2004) p.40 - p.43

Some men are born to watch over others (Armstrong, 2000). Indeed, the Kayan *Uma Pu* of the Apoh River Valley is what they are today because of the legacy left by their great leaders in the persons of *Penghulu Tama Paya Anyie, Penghulu Ajang Jok, Pemanca Laing Jok, and Headman Tama Anyi Avit.* These are the leaders of the *Kayan Uma Pu* that existed from the time of the British Colonial rule till the formation of Malaysia. Upon analysing these prominent leaders of the Kayan *Uma Pu*, one tends to realize that they are all part of the elaborate *Maren Uma* of the Kayan social class system. In essence, they are all part of the one big family of the Maren Kayan *Uma Pu* community. The kinship and the bond of the Kayan *Uma Pu* are cemented through the closely knit relationship of the *Maren Uma* of the *Kayan Uma Pu* of the Apoh region.

The emblem of authority:
The British government bestowed on Penghulu Tama Paya Anyie

No. 2 in B. 6/1   BMA   (BB)

                                    Marudi 22nd March,1946.

            TEMPORARY SURAT KUASA
            ****

        TAMA PAYA ANYKI USANG has been appointed
    PENGHULU of the Kayans in the Sungai Apoh (This
    does not include Rumah Oyong Deng at the mouth
    of the Apoh river.)

                                    .... Major.
                            C. A. O. - Marudi.

سورت كواس سمنتارا

تاما فايا' اڤيـخ اوسڠ ادد لنتق

منجاءي ڤڠهولو كايان ددالم سوڠي

اڤوه (اين تيدق دماصدق) ووماه

اويعڠ ديڠ دكوالا سوڠي اڤوه

The first appointment letter of Penghulu Tama Paya Anyie by the British government

TAMA PAYA ANYIE USUNG - [the right spelling] was appointed the PENGHULU of the Kayan Uma Pu of Apoh River on 22nd March 1946 and retired on 30th June 1974. Penghulu Tama Paya Anyie has left a legacy of being passionate, compassionate and protector of his people. He is nonetheless, brave and fearless in dealing with the British who govern the Baram at that time. In fact he was being used by the then British administration to assist in meeting and convincing the people to accept British rule. When the District Officer Mr. Griffin visited the Akah River during the beginning of 1949, Tama Paya Anyie was brought along to accompany him. He was indeed held in high esteem by the Brooke regime and the British Colonial government that control Sarawak then.

Penghulu Tama Paya Anyie was instrumental in getting the Kayans to embraced Christianity. Based on the account of Hudson Southwell, the people of Long Atip converted to Christianity on 10th March 1949. Prior to this, Southwell and his wife Winsome were in Long Tebangan of Akah River. They left Long Tebangan on 1st March 1949, and arrives Long Atip five days later which was on 6th March 1949.

How the villagers of Long Atip converted to Christianity were a most trying, frightening and apprehensive moment, especially to Penghulu Tama Paya Anyie - being both the leader of the people and a *'dayong'* or Shaman. Although he invited Southwell to Long Atip, he was not only fighting hard to convince the people, but more so with himself - fighting and struggling to denounce his spirit world. The accounts of Southwell about the conversion of the people of Long Atip were as follows:

> *"Penghulu Tama Paya Anyi welcomed us warmly to his spacious apartment in the longhouse, but told us he had many concerns. Although he was a dayong himself, there were others more deeply involved in the powers of the spirit world than he was, and they were reluctant or fearful to lose their occult powers and prestige. The Penghulu called several meetings of the people where the Southwell's could tell them of God's good news of deliverance from the powers of evil.*
>
> *After three days, the Penghulu again called the people together - about five hundred in all - and they affirmed their desire to follow Jesus Christ and cease worshipping the spirits. And the Penghulu solemnly spoke to spirits and informed them that he was no longer serving them or looking for them for their magic powers. Forthwith, he said, was serving the Almighty God alone."*

Southwell (1999) P. 273 - 274

Imagine the book of Ezra chapter 3:11 came alive amongst the Kayans of Long Atip: *'And they sang responsively, praising and giving thanks to the Lord: For He is good, for His mercy endures forever toward "Israel"* - the [**Kayan Uma Pu**]. *Then all the people shouted with great shout when they praise the Lord because the foundation of the house of the Lord was laid'.* [Ezra 3:11 – *'Lun nyanyi nah daha', pehu'ei-pehu'ei lemken mahek Tuhan dahin bara sayu kenep men Iha' nunih,*

> *"Tuhan, Iha' nah aleng sayu,*
> *halam Na' aleng paen atih peletu em*
> *tei ketapah te' kelunan 'Israel' [Kayan Uma Pu] nih".*

Lim daha' medeng aya alem daha' mahek aran Tuhan, avin bato' tuvu Uma Tuhan anan uh en daha' tegereng'.

Thus, the crucial and bold step taken by Penghulu Tama Paya Anyie saw all the **Kayan Uma Pu** become Christians of the Borneo Evangelical Mission denomination today. Prior to becoming Christians, the Kayans of Apoh River were practicing animistic, occult and magical powers. Their lives were controlled by all sorts of mystical and spiritual powers that made them always live in fear and uncertainty each day of their life. Certain birds and animals have strong influence on their lives and beliefs.

Picture: Penghulu Tama Paya Anyie is first on the right. Penghulu Ajang Jok is third from the left, with Tama Anyie Avit first on the left.

And the moment of Exodus 34: 6 - 9 was real to the people as well, *'And the Lord passed before him and proclaimed, "The Lord, the Lord God, merciful and gracious, longsuffering and abounding in goodness and truth. Keeping mercy for thousands, forgiving iniquity and transgression and sin, by no means clearing the guilty, visiting the iniquity of the fathers upon the children and the children's children to the third and fourth generation. If now I have found grace in your sight, o Lord, let my Lord, I pray, go among us, even though we are a stiff-necked people; and pardon our iniquity and our sin, and take us as your inheritance'.* [Usang Daha' Israel 34: 6 - 9: *'Lun panau nah Tuhan unan Musa pelalau kuma', "Akui nah Tuhan, Tuhan, Akui nah Allah aleng nyalam dahin masi, aru kenep, nyungei asi dahin teneng lan, aleng petageng jaji Kui dahin libu-libu' kelunan, dahin mebet kenep aleng mahing, dahin mebet dusa nun-nun. Bi daha' aleng sala adeng kui mukum daha'. Akui nyulei sala taman daha' ateng anak daha' nurei pah ateng sau-sau daha' dahin ateng tebin daha' aleng ketelo' dahin kepat. Ken na' "U Tuhan, iha' Ika lan masi akui, akui akei Ika' nei panau tugung kame, Im ala nah kame, jadi daven Ka tua", ken Musa.*

As such, Penghulu Tama Paya Anyie has left a legacy of hope to the *Kayan Uma Pu* which should be sustained and upheld by his children, grandchildren and the *Kayan Uma Pu* specifically for the betterment, prosperity and wellness of living of the Kayan tribe generally. Penghulu Tama Paya Anyie has shown his true and highest quality of leadership when he led the Kayans of Apoh to embrace Christianity. This also showed his true grit of *Kayan Maren Uma* that put the interest and importance of his people above self-interest. His boldness and concern for his people was revealed and related to Southwell as follows:

> *"The last time I met you it was in opposition to the message you brought. Now I have seen what it has done for other Kayan people. Please, will you come to my people in the Apoh and bring the message from God"*

Southwell (1999) P. 273

Hudson and Winsome Southwell - Source: Family Album

Therefore, the agreement, instruction and authority of Penghulu Tama Paya Anyie Usung, to get the Kayans to embraced Christianity opened the floodgates of blessings, change and transformation to the lives, future and security of the *Kayan Uma Pu* that are indeed blessed today.

Looking back to the past 64 years from the time of the early missionaries until now, the Kayan Uma Pu is indeed a very special and blessed tribe. Our blessings are countless and overflowing. There are 16 people that have become fulltime pastors and workers from Long Atip until today.

GOD'S GRACE, MERCY AND DELIVERANCE WAS POURED UPON THE KAYAN UMA PU TRIBE ON 10TH MARCH 1949

Poster: God's abundant grace and blessings upon the Kayan Uma Pu

Sons of Penghulu Tama Paya Anyie: (Left) Deng Anyie TK Long Bemang
and Kalang Anyie Former TK Long Atip (Right)

Prior to becoming Christian, Penghulu Tama Paya Anyie Usung was bestowed the name *'Jelivan'*. *Jeliva*n is indeed a name that fit and accorded to a man of power and authority. In his time then, Penghulu Tama Paya Anyie was powerful, fearful, mystical and magical in authority for he was also a *'dayong'* or shaman. *Jelivan* in the Kayan tribe means King Cobra, the most poisonous of all snakes of which the Kayans of power and authority are fondly associated with as a mean to express and exert authority. When Penghulu Tama Paya Anyie Usung embraced Christianity, he maintained the name *'Anyie'* and totally discarded the name 'Jelivan' from his personal record and identity. And his present off springs is totally unaware of this matter.

AJANG JOK in the centre of the picture, the headman of Long Bemang, was appointed PENGHULU of Kayan *Uma Pu* TELANG USAN on 1st July 1974, to replace Tama Paya Anyie who retired, and *Ajang Jok* was Penghulu until 19th June 1993, when he passed away. Prior to this, *Penghulu Ajang Jok* was offered the Penghulu post twice, but each time he rejected it because he followed the advice of his late father Penghulu Tama Wan Baya, who felt that it was not appropriate to have two Penghulus for the Kayan *Uma Pu* which may split the kinship and cohesiveness of the Kayan *Uma Pu* ethnic group.

Health Department staff photo with Penghulu Ajang Jok

Penghulu Ajang Jok has to agree to the third offer of Penghulu post as he was mindful of the sincerity of the government. Penghulu Ajang Jok felt that he should not offend the government anymore that may also imply that the Kayan *Uma Pu* generally, is not cooperating with the government. Indeed, it was most appropriate that he be given the post as he was the most eligible and qualified to the post.

The spirit of humbleness tends to get the better of the Penghulu, which is inherent in the Kayan community generally. This also reflects on the noble spirit of the *Maren Uma* that is not proud but shoulders their responsibility in all honesty and sincerity. *Ajang Jok* has been the headman of Long Bemang *Kayan Uma Pu* in the early 1940s. *Ajang Jok* also has held the distinguished post of Councillor of Baram District Council from 1963 that he relinquished upon being appointed Penghulu. Simultaneously, the post of headman was handed over to his son *Ngau Ajang*. *Ngau Ajeng* has been elevated to the Penghulu of The Kayan *Uma Pu*, and the Headman of Long Bemang was taken over by *Deng Anyie*, the second son of Penghulu Tama Paya Anyie who married one of the daughters of Penghulu Ajang Jok. *Deng Anyie or Taman Hunei Deng* has now retired and the position of headman is passed down to one of his sons, *Usung Deng*.

Picture: With Ketua Kampong Long Bemang Deng Anyie

AVIT LETCHU who is popularly known as **TAMA ANYIE AVIT** is a great Kenyah-Kayan leader in Long Wat of Apoh River. The founding of the present day Long Wat longhouse came about through the dynamic and capable leadership of Tama Anyie Avit. Tama Anyie Avit is a tall, tough and commanding figure befitting his stature as a leader and *Maren Uma*. Avit Letchu became entrenched into the *Maren Uma* when he married Paya Anyie, the eldest daughter of Penghulu Tama Paya Anyie Usung. Tama Anyie Avit was indeed a well-like man by his peers, nephews, nieces and the community at large due to his kindness and caring character. Tama Anyie Avit is indeed a man of fine character, humble, loving and always very concern for his family, relatives and the Kayan-Kenyah community of Apoh River valley. He is also a god-fearing man who is also active in Christian evangelical mission work. His famous and well-known brother is the late Dato' Sri Joseph Balan Seling, a former Minister in the State Government of Sarawak.

The people of Long Wat are a mix of Kenyah and Kayan groups. The Kenyah group are known to have come from the same namesake of Murum Belaga - they brought along the name to their present settlement in Apoh River. The Kenyahs are indeed a small community amongst the Kayans of Apoh. Nonetheless, they got amalgamated into the Kayan tribe after the marriage of one of the sons of the leaders of the Kenyahs, **Avit Letchu** to the eldest daughter of Penghulu Tama Paya Anyie Usung of Long Atip. As such, the Kenyahs became absorbed naturally into the greater and True-Kayan tribe of Apoh River. The dominance of the Kayans was reinforced by the influx of the

remnant or the last group of Kayan Uma Pu of Patah River valley to Long Wat in the early 1980s. This was made possible through the capable and respected leadership of *Tama Anyie Avit @ Avit Letchu*.

During his tenure as headman, both the Kenyah and Kayan groups were combined together at a new and the present longhouse site. Prior to that, the village of Long Wat was found at two separate locations of about 30 minutes apart by motor-boat ride - one site for the small Kenyah group and another site for the Kayan group. Thus, the present day Long Wat of Apoh River was established through the selfless effort, respectability and authority of Tama Anyie Avit @ Avit Letchu. Presently, his son *Anyie Avit or Taman Aren Anyie* is the headman of Long Wat.

Long Wat Headman Tama Anyie Avit @ Avit Letchu and his wife,
the eldest daughter of Penghulu Tama Paya Anyie Usung

Lunch at the house of TK Ingan Sang Long Bedian 1978

The leadership pattern in the *Kayan Uma Pu* is very distinct, entrenched and concrete. The leadership amongst the *Orang Ulu* that includes the Kayans is drawn up into various levels starting from the level of *Tua kampong* or headman at the village level. The next higher level is the *Penghulu* who is vested authority over several Tua Kampongs, and then moving up to the next level as *Pemanca* and finally the *Temenggong*, who is the Paramount Chief of the Orang Ulu communities. Thus, there is a leadership hierarchy that is inherent in the Kayan community and the Orang Ulu.

Nonetheless, how do we see ourselves as Kayan Uma Pu? And most importantly, how do other people see the Kayan Uma Pu? As has been made known by the early missionaries, the *Kayan Uma Pu* is more coordinated about their way of life. In the local dialect, it is translated as '*teneng lun urip Kayan Uma Pu*'. Their way of life and their spoken language is easier to follow and to speak. Thus, the Bible was translated into Kayan using the Kayan Uma Pu dialect. The *Kayan Uma Pu* is seen to be more refined and fine in character. The basic fundamental of the Kayan Uma Pu lies in their kinsmanship and their great respect for the '*Maren Uma*' or '*Hipun Uma*', that is expressed as, '*nusi hadau te' daha' hipun uma*'. Thus, there is always mutual respect and harmony between the '*hipun uma*' and the '*panyin*' - *murip piah, avin awi em te' panyin, nusi te' hipun uma* - that is translated as living harmoniously together because if there are no servants, there will be no master. This kind of altruistic values lies in the belief that the '*Maren Uma*' manages the life of the people - '*kelunan hipun uma mengatun urip*'.

Dialogue and interview: Defining the future of Kayan Uma Pu 'Maren Uma'

Therefore, the '*panyin*' should never '*nyile*" or seize, eliminate or erode the position of the '*Maren Uma*' or else *lali* or '*parit*' will befall them. The erosion and destruction of the Kayans and more so the Kayan Uma Pu social structure and fabric, lies in the rise and threat of new classes of '*Maren Uma*'. A case in point as pointed by a respected Kayan elder is the removal of Pemanca Laing Jok who is a '*Maren Uma*' whose leadership acumen and prowess is forgotten by the people. As reiterated: '*Sayu itam kelunan panyin nyineng katah - hadau tua te' Laing Jok (Pemanca), bi iha' aleng mengatun dahin dulung itam men'a'*. This kind of event should never have happened as it can have dire or grave consequences to the community.

Nevertheless, the '*Maren Uma*' needs to support, encourage and motivate each other. They have to be seen to be united as this will serve as pillar of strength in the *Kayan Uma Pu*. There is power in unity - '*Te' tingan awi piah kenep*'. When the '*Hipun Uma*' or '*Maren Uma*' walk in righteousness, their lives and those of their '*panyin*' will be blessed. Thus, for the *Kayan Uma Pu*, the '*Maren Uma*' will continue to be supported fully by the '*panyin*' for the common good of the tribe. There is the continued belief that the '*Maren Uma*' have the mystical power as the good spirit abides in them - '*Te' adat te' urip daha' Maren Uma, tok nilung te' daha*''. This is illustrated in the fact that the '*Maren Uma*' has the following powers: '*Tenangan urip*'; '*Awing tening*'; and '*Buring ketiggai*' which are comparable to Biblical interpretations that resembles as: Tuhan Allah - God; Tuhan Yesus - Jesus; and Roh Kudus - Holy Spirit. As is seen by the Kayan people generally, the Kayan leaders are '*lali*' or degraded from their original position as '*Maren Uma*'. Thus, they are seen to be ineffective in their position to protect and guard the rights of the people and sovereignty of the '*Maren Uma*'.

Maren Uma Long Bemang: TK Deng Anyie and Penghulu Ngau Ajeng

Long Bedian is a modern and developed Kayan village in the upper reaches of Sungai Apoh of Marudi District. Sungai Apoh is a tributary of Sungai Tutoh, which is one of the two main tributaries of the mighty Baram River. The village is accessible via Marudi town. From Marudi, one has to take an express boat to Long Lama, which will take about three hour's journey. And from Long Lama, a one-hour journey of inland logging track is taken to finally reach the village. An alternative inland journey from Miri can also be taken that takes between four to six hours going through Beluru, Lapok, Long Lama and onward to Long Bedian.

Long Bedian is seen to have a reputation as a 'developed' village. This makes the village a benchmark for the other villages in Sarawak. After having won numerous District, Division, State and the National visionary development awards, how will the people continue to sustain their interest, momentum, and efforts for continuous development? Upon winning the prestigious national visionary award and shouldering the name of '*best village*' (Borneo Post, May 9, 2002), will the people continue to sustain and maintain this 'developed' tag?

Long Bedian is a relatively progressive village that has won the National Village Visionary Development Award 2002. This tends to confirm the fact that Long Bedian is indeed a '*cut above the rest*' of the rural villages in Sarawak. Nonetheless, the question though, is this really so? In what area of advancement makes Long Bedian well above the rest of the rural villages not only in Sarawak but also in the whole nation of Malaysia? Indeed this has a lot to do with the capable leadership of **Laing Jok** who is the '*Maren Uma*' or headman of the village. He became the headman of the village in August 1985, succeeding his grandfather Taman Engan Sang who has passed away. He rose to become *Pemanc*a or Paramount Chief of the Kayans in May 2007 until 2011.

The good and capable leadership in the village is a significant factor that is able to unite the people. The leadership structure though is hereditary, is blended with general consensus for the other appointments in the committee. The young generations of second echelon leaders have moved to steer the community towards the transformation of the physical and economic progress of the village. The people themselves are very receptive to new changes and developments. The culture of *collectivism* (Triandis, 1994) and strong spirit of '*collective action*' is inherent in the community of Long Bedian. However, the development of the village tends to move in different interfaces especially in terms of the diverse and wide array of community developments projects that are supported and funded by the government and corporate bodies.

Nonetheless, continuous development should be seen as the peoples' initiative as well. Can't the people work on their own development activities or projects? Perhaps the people should be encouraged to become coordinators, implementers, evaluators and financiers of development projects in their village.

The people of Long Bedian have shown great interest in the continuous progress and development of their village. For instance, they are very keen for the Health Department to introduce the Healthy Village Programme. Nonetheless, it must be emphasized that the development of the village should be seen as a partnership of the villagers with the various government agencies, voluntary bodies, NGOs and or private individuals for a win-win situation.

Beautiful and friendly Kayan Uma Pu ladies of Long Bedian

Some Long Bedian folks: Do' Wan, Jok Engan, Ubung Ing, and Urai Jau

Pemanca Laing Jok's Parents: Jok Engan and Ubung Ing

A significant and progressive landmark of Long Bedian

4

The Kayan Longhouse

The most salient feature of the Kayan social organization is the practice of longhouse domicile. This is a structure supported by hardwood posts of the 'Belian' tree that can be hundreds of metres long and usually located along the river bank.

The Kayan villagers as a norm live under one roof in a communal house rather than in separate houses. Due to the very long stretch of the structure, it is termed as 'longhouse'. Each longhouse or 'Uma aru' as the Kayan called it may accommodate fifty or more families. The Kayan villages in Apoh River valley are amongst the longest and populated villages in Baram District and even in Sarawak for that matter. The 'Uma aru' stands on pillars of hardwood, usually the renowned ironwood or 'belian', and is elevated from eight to fifteen feet above the ground, with ironwood shingles for the roof.

In those old days, the longhouse is really a long straight structure on stilts, and is divided into one-room 'amin' (bilik) or compartment or door. Each of these single 'amin' accommodates one Kayan family, and there is but one access door to each 'amin'. Therefore, the capacity of a Kayan longhouse is determined by the number of doors found. For the Kayans in Apoh River the number of doors for each village is relatively big as per Table below. The longest and biggest village in Apoh River is Long Bemang.

Table: Villages door and population in Apoh River

Name of Village	Door	Population
Long Bemang	120	1074
Long Wat	69	623
Long Atip	115	1300
Long Bedian	113	1102

Source: Health Department, Marudi District. (2000)

The general construction design of those early Kayan village homes with those of the present is about the same. One ascends to them by means of a notched log or ladder at each end of the long balcony or veranda which extends the entire length of the longhouse. This outer veranda is open and is useful in drying of paddy, fish-nets, clothing and seasoning wood for carving. After the veranda but under the roof is the long hallway which also extends the entire length of the longhouse. Directly from this long hallway open the single doors into each separate living room or 'amin', occupied by the different families. Each family though, have their own house which is separated from another family by a completely sealed wooden wall.

A typical native longhouse showing the outer veranda

A native longhouse without the outer veranda

A typical native longhouse showing the outer veranda

A typical *Dayak* longhouse of the 1930s

The long hallway or thoroughfare is about twenty feet wide without any cross-partitions. One can simply goes up the ladder or notched log at one end, walks the entire length of hallway and down the ladder at the other end which is just like the village street. The outer gallery has no roof and is useful in drying paddy on mats placed on its floor in the burning sun. It is also serviceable in drying fish-nets, bleaching clothing, and seasoning wood for carving (Krohn, 1927; 2001).

This hallway or 'hawa' is often used as common area for socialization, and as living-room. The hallway is the tribal meeting place, especially at the hall of the village headman. Here the people convene before any important undertakings begun. It may be in reference to an expedition to collect rattan, 'damar' or *resins*, wild jeluotng sap or sago, or a discussion for starting the clearing of new land for paddy growing, merry making and celebrations. It is the village meeting place for the purposes of either business or pleasure.

The 'hawa' that is seen as the public hall stretches the whole length of the longhouse without any partition, it is cool and pleasant place, and is much frequented by men and women for conversation and indoor pursuits. Here the women often do their chores such as weaving baskets and beads, or plaiting of mats. Here too, the men chop up the firewood or even make boats if not of too great a size. As Gomes (1911) described it, *"the 'hawa' is a public place open to all comers, and used as a walk-way by travellers, who climb up the ladder at one end, walk through the whole length of the house,*

The longhouse built on strong rounded ironwood or belian tree posts.

The hallway of an old longhouse that was still found in 1979

and go down the ladder at the other end. *The floor is carpeted with thick and heavy mats, made of cane interlaced with strips of beaten bark. Over these are spread other mats of finer texture for visitors to sit upon".*

A longhouse hallway

A picture of the long hallway of a longhouse

VERANDAH OF A KAYAN HOUSE AT LONG LAMA, BARAM RIVER

Kayan longhouse: Haddon. A.C. (1932) - Headhunters: Black, white and brown.

This part of '*Uma Aru*' or longhouse hallway of Long Atip which comprises
88 doors is so long that the eye view could hardly see the end

A view of a portion of Long Bemang longhouse

A view of the middle row of Long Bedian longhouse

Maren Uma house in Long Bedian which is normally extended out

Long Wat longhouse 1978

In the old days, the posts of the long public hallway are often adorned with the horns of deer and tusks of wild boars and bears - trophies from the spoils of their hunting spears and dogs. On the side of the long hallway is a row of doors. Each of these leads into a separate room or *'amin'* which is occupied by each family. The doors open outwards, and each is closed by means of a heavy weight of stone secured by a thong fastened to the inside. This room or 'amin' serves several purposes. It serves as a kitchen, and in one corner there is a fireplace where the food is cooked. This fireplace is set against the wall of the veranda, and resembles an open cupboard. The lowest shelf rest on the floor, and is boarded all round and filled with earth. This forms the fireplace or *'avo"*, and is furnished with a few stones or round iron stand or 'angan' upon which the pots are set for cooking. The shelf immediately above the fireplace is set apart for smoking fish or meat. The shelves above are filled with firewood, which is thoroughly dried by the smoke and ready for use. As the smoke from the wood fire is not channelled through the roof by any kind of chimney, it spread itself through the loft, and blackens the beams and rafters of the roof.

The avo' or fireplace of a family kitchen · Cooking Rice

The *'amin'* also serves as a dining-room. When the food is ready, mats are spread, and the family members' squat on the floor to eat their meal. There is no furniture, the floor serving the dual purpose of table and chairs. The 'amin' also serves as a bedroom. At night the mats for sleeping on are spread out and the mosquito nets hung up. There is no window to let in the air and light, but a portion of the roof is so constructed that it can be raised a foot or two, and kept open by means of a pole or stick. Round the three sides of the room are arranged the treasured valuables such as old jars, brass gongs and guns. Their cups and plates are hung up in rows flat against the walls. The flooring is the same as the veranda, which is made from split palm, bamboo or hewn timber that may be fastened down with rattan or nailed. The floor is swept after a task, the refuse falling through the flooring to the ground underneath. Nonetheless, the '*amin*' is often stuffy, and not such a pleasant place as the open veranda. The pigs and poultry occupy the waste space under the house.

From the '*amin*' there is a ladder which leads to an upper room or loft or '*parung*', where they kept their tools and store their paddy baskets or '*ingen*', which the Kelabits called '*bu'an*' and '*binen*'. If the family is a large one, the young unmarried girls sleep in the loft, the boys and young men sleeping outside in the veranda.

The modern day Kayan longhouses still resembles those past villages in terms of architectural plan and construction design. Nonetheless, they are now mostly built on the ground. The open hall way is still present. After the hall way, separated by a wall is the living-room. The sleeping rooms are found on the upper floor of each '*amin*' or '*bilik*'.

A view of the upper part of Long Atip as seen from the middle of the village

5

Rich cultural heritage of the Kayans

Culture is seen as the customs and civilization of a particular people or group. In every society of the world, there is some uniqueness of the way of life of the people. Thus, the Kayan people of the Apoh region of Baram district are no exception. This can be seen in the day to day way of life of the people. The uniqueness of the cultures of the people is best seen in their dances, traditional dress, costumes, music, beliefs, and their environment. There are different types of cultures across the world and each culture has its unique essence. While defining the term 'culture', there are several elements that together constitute as the culture of a particular region or the culture of particular people. We fail to understand what the elements of a culture are, but we can learn more by looking through these terms:

- *Language*: The various languages are essentially an important part of the culture.

- *Norms*: Every society or every civilization has a set of norms, which are an inseparable part, and an important element of the culture. This can include the folkways, mores, taboos and rituals in a culture.

- *Values*: The social values of a particular civilization are also considered as an element of the culture. The values of a culture often refer to the things to be achieved or the things, which are considered of great worth or value in a particular culture.

- *Religion and Beliefs*: The religion and the beliefs of the people in a civilization play an important role in shaping up of the culture as well.

- **Social Collectives**: Social collectives refer to the social groups, organizations, communities, institutions, classes, and societies, which are considered as symbolic social constructions.

- **Status and Role in Society**: A status or a social role is nothing but a slot or position within a group or society, which gives an overall idea of the social structure and hence is an important element of culture. This can also include traditional gender-based or age-based roles.

- **Cultural Integration**: This includes the degree of harmony or integration within the various elements of culture. This can include elements like sub-cultures, local cultures and the difference between historical and cultural traditions.

As Neubeck and Glasberg (2005) pointed, culture is a complex system of behaviour, values, beliefs, traditions and artefacts, which is the social construction of reality of society's dominant groups, often imposed as a shared way of life among members of a society. Therefore, it is important to discover the meaning of culture, and its significance in the life of an individual and society. Without culture, and the relative freedom it signifies, society which is seen as perfect is but a multitude of selfish individuals. As such, any authentic creation that becomes a part or a way of life is a gift to the future.

Why is culture important?

How do cultural values impact the way we live? Culture in this context refers to the pattern of human way of life and the signs, which give significance to those pursuits. Culture is manifested through the art, literature, costumes, customs and traditions of a community. Different cultures exist in different parts of the world. For instance, the natural environment greatly affects the lifestyles of the people of that region, thus shaping their culture. The diversity in the cultures around the world is also a result of the mindsets of people inhabiting different regions of the world. Why is culture important? Let us try to find out. The cultural values of a community give it an identity of its own. A community gains a character and a personality of its own, because of the culture of its people. Culture is shared by the members of a community. It is learned and passed from the older generations to the newer ones. For an effective transfer of culture from one generation to another, it has to be translated into symbols, (Neubeck and Glasberg, 2005). Thus, language, art and religion serve as the symbolic means of transfer of cultural values between generations.

The Kayan tribe generally has their unique, structured, and well defined way of life that becomes entrenched as a culture. Culture ties the people of a region or community together, that one common bond - which brings the people together. Thus, the customs and traditions that the people of a community follow, the festivals they celebrate, the kind of clothing they wear, the food they eat, and most importantly, the cultural values they adhere to, bind them together. Culture is seen as a system of social norms, wherein people shape their limits, standards and behaviour. The cultural values form the foundation of one's fundamental principles of life to the extent that they influence one's principles and philosophies of life. They influence one's way of living and thus impact social life. Thus, the cultures of the Kayans reflect the noble values and significance as discussed above. This can be seen from the ways of life of the Kayans in Apoh River valley and the Kayans of Long Atip particularly. Numerous programmes and activities were organized to revive, reinvent and sustain the cultures of the Kayan people, in the village of Long Atip. The Kayans of Long Bemang and Long Bedian do have regular traditional and cultural festivities as well.

Culture as a way of life

Culture is argued as a learned pattern of behaviour, which is a way how people live his life. It is an integral part of every society, and creates a feeling of belonging and togetherness among the people of that society. Culture encompasses various aspects of communication, attitude, etiquette, beliefs, values, customs, norms, food, art, jewellery, clothing styles, and other facets of life. Every society has a different culture, which gives it an identity and uniqueness. In spite of the vast cultural diversity, there are certain elements of culture that are universal though. They are known as cultural accomplishments that comprise certain behavioural traits and patterns that are inherent and common in all cultures around the world. For instance, classifying relations, having some form of art and music, use of jewellery, classifying people according to gender and age, for example, are common in all cultures of the world. 'Culture' is considered to be a complex term nonetheless, and a variety of anthropologists and researchers have defined it in various ways. Some of these definitions as outlined by Neubeck and Glasberg (2005) are: (1). Culture is that complex whole which includes knowledge, belief, art, morals, law, customs and other capabilities and habits acquired by man as a member of society; (2). Culture embraces all the manifestations of social habits of a community, the reactions of the individual as affected by the habits of the group in which he lives, and the product of human activities as determined by these habits; (3). Culture is what makes you a stranger when you're away from home; (4). Culture is a well-organized unity divided into two fundamental aspects - a body of artefacts and a system of customs; (5). Culture is the collective programming of the mind distinguishing the members of one group or category of people from another.

Culture nonetheless, can be acquired from the people surrounding us, our parents, guardians, relatives, and peers. This is always seen in the distinct set of beliefs, values, traditions and behaviour is passed over through generations. This is a collective phenomenon, and cannot exist in isolation in a single individual. It is shared at various levels, namely regional, local, gender, community, corporate, social class, and groups, but is also rich in diversity. Citizens of a nation share certain aspects of cultures, whereas different regions within a nation have their own unique blend of beliefs, values and styles, and way of life. Culture is cumulative and dynamic. The culture of any particular group is constantly evolving and undergoing insidious changes and modification. Each generation brings along a new set of changes and developments in the culture of that society. Moreover, long-term exposure to different cultures leads to the exchange of certain cultural transition, practices and modification.

What is the Significance of culture?

Culture is that invisible bond that ties the people of a society together. This refers to the pattern of societal livelihood strategies. For instance, the art, literature, language and religion of a community represent the community's culture. Culture manifests itself through the lifestyle of the individuals of a community. The moral values of the people for example, represent the culture of the community. The importance of culture is central to its close connection with the daily life pattern of the people. Different cultures of the world have created the diverse ways of life of the people inhabiting different parts of the globe.

The knowledge and experiences necessary for survival, and adaptation to our natural and social environment evolves and is acquired to form a culture. Culture is what imbibes into us the knowledge of good and bad, acceptable and non-acceptable norms and socializing characteristics. Consciously or unconsciously, it plays a significant role in shaping our personality and behaviour. Each individual has a distinct and unique personality. However, within a group, there exist certain regularities set patterns of norms in their behaviour. This can be attributed to the culture in which they grow up. In addition, culture also influences our perception of reality and worldly concepts. Our interpretations of the actions and events around us are moulded by our culture. It shapes the basic foundation of our life and behaviour.

As Armstrong (1995), Daft (2000) emphasized, culture is related to the development of one's attitude. One's culture plays an important role in shaping the principles of the individual's life.

Generally, the cultural values of an individual have a deep impact on his or her attitude towards life. As the proverb says, train a child in the way he should go and when he is old, he will not depart from it. According to behavioural studies perspective, definition of culture is seen as the ultimate system of social control where people monitor their own standards and behaviour (Neubeck and Glasberg, 2005). A community's culture lays the foundation of the way of life of its people. The cultural values serve as the founding principles of one's life. They shape an individual's thinking and influence his or her thinking style. Indeed, culture gives an individual a unique identity. The culture of a community gives its people a character of their own. Culture shapes the personality of a community. The language that a community speaks, the art forms it hosts, its staple food, its customs, traditions and festivities comprise the community's culture. Thus, the culture of the Kayan Uma Pu is still inherent in its spoken language, customs, traditions and festivities. The importance of culture cannot be stressed enough as it is an integral part of living. The challenges facing the culture of the Kayan Uma Pu are indeed imminent and real due to greater integration of the community with the other communities in the country and globally.

6

Beliefs and Omens of the Kayan tribe

According to Hose and McDougall (1912),[1] *the Kayans believe themselves to be surrounded by many intelligent powers capable of influencing their welfare for good or ill. Some of these are embodied in animals or plants, or are closely connected with other natural objects, such as mountains, rocks, rivers, caves; or manifest themselves in such processes as thunder, storm, and disease, the growth of the crops and disasters of various kinds. There can be no doubt that some of these powers are conceived anthropomorphically; for some of them are addressed by human titles, are represented by carvings in human form, and enjoy, in the opinion of the Kayans, most of the characteristically human attributes. Others are conceived more vaguely, the bodily and mental characters of man are attributed to them less fully and definitely; and it is probably true to say that these powers, all of which, it would seem, must be admitted to be spiritual powers - if the word spiritual is used in a wide sense as denoting whatever power is fashioned in the likeness of human will and feeling and intelligence. These ranges from the anthropomorphic being to the power which resides in the seed grain and manifests itself in its growth and multiplication, and which seems to be conceived merely as a vital principle, virtue, or energy inherent in the grain, rather than as an intelligent and separable soul'.*

The belief in the spirit world has been the central part of the lives of the indigenous tribes of Borneo in the past. The bird omens for instance, do have a strong influence on the natives of Sarawak in the past. This is indeed true to the Kayan tribe. The bird omens are not the same everywhere though. Certain birds or '*manuk*' have the greatest influence on the lives of the people. These birds normally used at night, are supposed to give the information being asked of them.

It is not only the cry of birds that the Kayans pay attention to. There are certain animals - the deer, armadillo, lizard, bat, python, cobra, even the rat, as well as certain insects - which all give omens under different and special circumstances. But these other creatures are subordinate to the birds, from which alone augury is sought at the beginning of any important undertaking (Gomes, 1911).

The tradition concerning the origin of bird-omens is that, 'in the beginning, a Dayak got married to a '*Tok*' or spirit, who conceived and brought forth the birds, which novel progeny being 'half-Dayaks' were cared and cherished by their paternal relatives till they could fend for themselves; and ever since they have shown their gratitude to the descendants of their quondam protectors by exercising the spiritual powers which they have derived from their mother, the '*Tok*' or '*hantu*', on their behalf, giving them warning of coming sickness or misfortune, and encouraging them to proceed in such undertakings as will end in advantage. Consequently, on every occasion of importance, the birds are taken into the confidence of the Kayans, and their advice is strictly adhered to. It may sound strange to say that 'in the beginning, men and spirits were on equal standings, and could eat, drink, and if necessary fight together. In those days, spirits were not hidden from mortal gaze, and men were not afraid of them.

The 'birds of the day' the '*isit*' and '*nyiho*' are consulted with respect to the good or evil fortune for every journey of importance. For instance, a '*dayong*' or shaman will chant and invoke the bird or '*manuk*' as follows: 'Hail O ancestors! O '*manuk*' cry on the left hand, and then make answer on the right; keep off rain, keep off wind, keep off darkness, keep off mist. Thou art the clever one, the long sighted one; keep off from us sharp things; keep off from us pointed things; keep off rain-storms; keep off wind-storms (Roth, 1968).

Accordingly, if the bird cry is first heard on the left hand, and then responded to on the right, all is well, good luck is certain; if heard in other directions, it is a sign that no success will result from the journey. In certain birds, if the sound is in front, go no further for sickness or death are waiting there; if behind, return at once or during absence, some deadly evil will come to the family or village.

The 'birds of night' are consulted regarding each year's farming, the locality of new houses, and for disputes between two people. The farming consultation for example, is done as follows: A likely spot is first located where a small hut is built. At night, the '*dayong*' with the elders who are appointed to conduct the ritual, go and seat them in the hut. The '*dayong*' cast into the air a little stained yellow rice and crying out loud, 'Hail, O ancestors! I wish to make enquiry about this spot of jungle; grant us here to make our farms, to do our work, grant here our paddy, our corns, our vegetables may live; let them be fat and good and flourishing. Let them be lucky, let them be successful; grant us long life to make our farms, to do our work. Fly from in front past us who are here; utter your cries, and give us an answer'. When the invocation is finished, the response is awaited. If the birds cry at a distance in front, and then fly past the hut and twitter among the trees behind it, the spot may be farmed. However, if the birds fly, cry and alight roundabout and near the hut without passing on, there are many spirits in that place, and to farm there would be to invite sickness, or death, or a bad crop.

The cries of the owl or '*manuk wak*', the hawk or 'nyiho', and of a small kind of frog called '*tunum*', if heard at night by those who are on their way to consult the birds, are an omen of evil, and a warning to stop or cease for that night. Again if the cry of an owl or hawk be heard by a party on the war-path, in the direction which the head-hunters are about to take, they must return, or shame and loss will be the outcome of their expedition. Again if the cry of the three kind of deer found in Sarawak be heard, when starting on a journey, or when going to consult the birds by day or by night, it is a sign that, if the matter in hand is followed up, sickness will befall the group. Also, if a newly married couple hear them at night, they must be divorced as this is not done, the death of the bride or bridegroom will occur.

There are other creatures besides birds whose sound of warning they observe. A cobra or '*jelivan*' crossing the path compels the return of the advancing party. A rat on the farm is also the same. A '*tela'uh*' or wild deer, when heard on the hill near the farms sends all the people home. A deer crying at night keeps all at home the next day. A kind of grasshopper sounding at night is a sign of a healthy house but should it go no till dawn, no one is to go out. To hear the cry of a deer is at all times unlucky. On the way to the farms, should any unlucky omens be heard, the people will return home and do no more work for the day (Roth, 1968).

In the old days, the indigenous tribes that included that Kayans of both men and women are hardworking people. However, much economic loss was encountered because of time wasted in observing the various feasts on the tribal calendar, as well as for consultation of an almost endless list of signs and omens. On this account, (Krohn, 1927; 2001) is of the view that less than one third of their annual activities was devoted to actual work pursuits.

The impact of bad omens was badly felt by the various indigenous tribes in the past. For instance, a paddy field that was cleared from the jungle by the hardest kind of labour such as the felling of trees, clearing of logs and ready for planting was completely given up because of the appearance of bad omen. Thus, depriving an entire longhouse of rice so necessary for food, causing hardships and suffering of famine or '*liyen*" that would not have happened but for the inexorable superstitions that gripped the lives of the people for many generations (Krohn, 1927; 2001).

A succession of bad misfortunes, such as repeated bad paddy harvest or the outbreak of an epidemic of disease, is regarded as a clear sign to the entire village that evil spirits have prevailed over the good spirits which must be taken as a certain indication that the entire village must be moved to a new location. The site on which to build a new longhouse is indeed a very difficult decision. Many things must be taken into consideration, such as the character of the land, proximity to water, the availability of suitable lands in the vicinity for paddy fields, and most importantly the signs of good fortune is brought back by the good spirits.

Thus the lives of the Kayans in the past or before the middle of the 1940s were very much influenced by the powers of the birds and animals. The mystical and spiritual powers in those days were real and frightening. With the bold and courageous step taken by the *Kayan Maren Uma* around the middle of 1940s, the Kayans and especially the *Kayan Uma Pu* of the Apoh valley have totally abandoned the animistic and spirit beliefs of the past. The gamble and bold move by *Penghulu Tama Paya Anyie* to get the people of Long Atip and the *Kayan Uma Pu* specifically, to embrace Christianity on 10th March, 1949, has released the people from the bondage of fear and uncertainty, to the life of hope, peace and security.

7

Understanding the migration phenomenon: The Homecoming Events of *Hituk* or Honouring the home-place

The people of Apoh River and much so in Long Atip, have always been living in harmony and solidarity. The excellent cooperation and cohesiveness in the community has created a bond of togetherness and brotherhood amongst the people. This is a culture that is inherent in the Kayan community that has been passed from generation to generation. This culture of cooperation and cohesiveness has been a pillar of strength towards the progress and development of the community over the years.

There are numerous cultures of cooperation, cohesiveness and kinsmanship amongst the Kayan community. All forms of community activities and programmes rest heavily on these beautiful, fantastic and altruistic values and comradeship of the Kayans. The daily life of the Kayans is imbued in these rich cultural practices.

What motivates and stirs up the idea of '*Hituk Long Atip*' or *honouring the home-place*, was the phenomenon of movement of the people to the towns and cities in Sarawak and Malaysia, and beyond. The unusual and absurd movements of the people were the fact that the whole members of the family leave their home. Thus, one can imagine what will become of the house condition? Naturally this led to the feeling of concern and worry towards the 'wandering' people of Long Atip as well as the poor state of their untended houses. This has created or caused to emanate numerous socio-economic implications that were detrimental to the sustainability of progress and development of the village in the long term.

The migration of a whole family for instance, caused the house to be abandoned and neglected for most part of the year. In some cases families never returned home anymore. The burden of getting the people to return home has become more pressing and necessary. Thus, the idea of organizing a festival was mooted to entice the people home. As such, a carnival "*Hituk Long Atip*" or "*Remembering the peace, harmony and prosperity of Long Atip*" towards its sons and daughters was organized. The first carnival "*Hituk Long Atip*" was organized from 23rd November to 25th November 1995. This inaugural event to get the sons and daughters of Long Atip to return home showed a tremendous response and success.

The objectives of the carnival '*Honouring Long Atip Village*' were:

1. As part of the continuous endeavour of the sons and daughters of Long Atip and in tandem with the '*Youth Friendship Programme*' of the government, there is a need to synergize the future generations to strive for the realization of Vision 2020 founded upon the following challenges:

   - To contribute to the creation of a united Malaysia through a shared vision with other communities.

   - To establish a community that have an open spirit that embraces peace and progress that exudes self confidence, proud of our achievements and brave to face challenges.

   - To establish a community that has a caring culture.

2. To keep alive the indebtedness, consciousness and awareness of the community towards past leaders and elders that has contributed towards the development of Long Atip.

3. To instil and establish the spirit of gratitude amongst the community towards the elders and leaders in all aspects of village and community development, especially the inheritance of cultures through the generations till the present time.

4. To propel the community towards the remembrance of the prudence and selfless service of the elders and village leaders of Long Atip.

Chairman of "*Hituk Long Atip*" festival 1995 Nawan Luhat, delivering his welcoming and appreciation address.

Some of the participants' show-casing the rich culture of its people.

The need to preserve the unique cultures of the Kayan community of Long Atip has always been the desires and aspiration of the elders and leaders. The Kayans of Long Atip do indeed have a rich cultural heritage that has been preserved and maintained through the generations. Certain cultures nonetheless, were on the decline and seldom practiced or used due to the changing times and modification of life style. If these are not preserved or practiced, may one day be lost or become extinct. Thus, the people of the village are enticed home through the celebration of the rich cultures of the *Kayan Uma Pu* by means of the 'homecoming events'.

Appreciation to *Mr. Leo Maekiaho* for his contributions to the '*Hituk Long Atip*' festival

An elaborate programme of games, fun, cultural performances and '*Pah lung*' or community get together, was drawn over a period of four days. There was always an opportunity for everyone to get involved and participated in the numerous activities organized.

The village was divided into three groups that comprised of around about 40 doors each. This provided an avenue for the people to contribute teams and members to participate in all the games and other programmes organized. The spirit of friendly competition was created to add creativity, originality and coordinated presentations by everyone.

As can be seen from the various pictures taken, there were indeed the varied arrays of traditional costumes, head gears, musical instruments, music, dances, crafts and other artefacts that reflected the rich culture and ways of life of the Kayan community. For instance, the Orang Ulu traditional warrior costume came in various colours, beauty and designs that fascinated and enthralled everyone. These sorts of traditional attires has become a legacy of their past that is still cherished and kept as a culture by the Kayan community of Long Atip.

The costumes, music and dances depict and portray the ways of life of the forefathers of the Kayan community. The mystique, mystery and fascination of the life and culture of the Kayans of the past came alive to the new generations.

The programmes that were organized covered a wide variety of games, and traditional activities. The activities that reflected an atmosphere of fun, merriment and conviviality showed the cohesiveness and well entrenched and inherent values and rich cultures of the people. The programmes included activities like:

- '*Nyivan Lasan*' or single dance for men and women.
- Telematch competition.
- *Sape* music competition
- '*Nyivan pekatah*' or sketch dance.
- '*Dak selingut*' or flute music competition.
- '*Tekna*' or traditional legend song.
- '*Nyivan Sau Kayau*' or '*Tawak*' music dance.
- '*Nyivan upah*' to reflect traditional attires and lifestyle.
- '*Pagan Tawak*' or Gong musical Beat.
- '*Nyivan joh*' or long dance.
- '*Pah lung*' or village get-together party.

Homecoming events were organized every two years since 1995. The homecoming event of Long Atip 2005 although not elaborate in terms of preparation was a roaring success. The modest preparation was met with enthusiastic response and participation by everyone. Various activities were organized as part of the Christmas and year-end celebration. The activities kicked-off with the village picnic to *Kaka'* Lake. The event was made more synergistic by the presence of the Honourable *Lihan Jok*, the State Legislative Council representative of Telang Usan. In spite of his very busy schedule, he made it a point to come to Long Atip, to be with the people. This made the spirit of '*Homecoming Long Atip 2005*' a fine example that should be emulated by the sons and daughters of Long Atip. Everyone should have the passion to return home wherever possible each year.

Towards this end, an annual event was organized in Long Atip to foster the homecoming spirit and nurturing the love and passion to return home. The rich culture and heritage of the people of Long Atip should be presented and celebrated to create a festive, merriment and convivial atmosphere during this annual event.

The '*Homecoming Long Atip 2005*' was a fine example that showed everyone that was present participated wholeheartedly to the traditional and cultural events that were organized. Can anyone imagine the whole village of hundreds of people joining and lining themselves for the '*Nyivan upah*'? This was what happened in Long Atip. Therefore, it is possible that this kind of cultural event, can be promoted as a tourism package to the outside world.

The homecoming events continued to be celebrated every year since 2005. The people have seen the uniqueness and conviviality of the celebrations. The homecoming events have become a yearly attraction that showcase the rich cultural heritage of the Kayans.

Kayan beauties of Long Atip dress in their traditional costumes

Why do people move? Kosinski & Prothero (1975) are of the view that migration takes place when an individual decides that it is preferable to move rather than to stay and where the difficulties of moving seem to be more than offset by the expected rewards. This tend to indicate that movements generally take place in response to the circumstances, actual as well as potential and perceived, with which people are faced both in their home communities and in areas away from home. The problems, opportunities and changes associated with the development process provide the motivation for the movement initiative. Migration though, is usually preceded by a process of decision-making in which the advantages and disadvantages are carefully weighed up, and where the potential difficulties associated with migration may be traded off against those which might result from staying put.

Movements of people are a phenomenon for various groups, ethnics and populations across the globe. This though, has caught up with the people of the village of Long Atip in the 1980s that was seen as unusual in the tribe. Nevertheless, this can be seen as a culture similar to that of the Iban *'bejalai'* - wandering and venturing on journeys and trips to seek employment and fortunes in the towns. A key aspect of many forms of population movement like rural-urban migration is that they offer the frustrating hope of better prospects elsewhere, but that these often fail to materialize in reality.

On a global scale, the movement and interaction of people through history has been an important factor in world civilization, in the enrichment of cultures and the diversification of technology; migration being an integral and vital part of human development (Bilsborrow, et al, 1984). There is no simple explanation to suggest an answer to the extraordinary scale to population movements that is both actual and latent. Nonetheless, Parnwell (1993) is of the view that this may be attributed to one or more of the following factors:

- The failure of the process of economic growth to bring about an even pattern of development in which all areas, sectors and groups of people have shared to a more or less equal measure.

- The penetration of the market economy has also strongly underpinned the movement of people. Thus out-migration to seek paid employment may represent the best means of obtaining an income with which to satisfy these growing cash needs and people's rising aspirations with regard to preferred standard of living.

- The process of modernization and social change have been important in underpinning the growth of population movements from the rural areas to urban centres, which is rather difficult to isolate cause from effect. Education though, has proven to be a powerful instrument of social change that has the effect of raising people's qualifications and expectations beyond the capacity of their home areas to accommodate.

- The rapid pace of population growth provides added momentum to the rate of population movements. An example is the failure or inability to accommodate population growth by expanding the cultivated area or intensifying agricultural practices.

- Population growth may push land-hungry communities into fairly marginal ecological zones such as infertile uplands, riverine areas which may be prone to flooding or dry arid areas which may face prolong period of droughts.

- People may have to leave their homes to make way for infrastructural projects such as reservoirs, ports, roads, hydro dams and so forth.

- And people throughout the world have been displaced from their home areas by various forms of persecutions and strife. The nature of political regime which governs the country may also make the position of certain groups of people in their societies untenable.

For the Kayans of Apoh, movements are due to several fundamental processes that underpin the mobility of the people. Some of the obvious factors includes the following: increasing demand and opportunities for tertiary education; the changes in the position of women into greater accountability and responsibility for the family; the changing relationship and division of responsibility between parents and children; better access to medical and health services; and more so in the context of '*melei ilau kuman*' - easier to make or earn a living. Even in most cases though, there is often an economic motive behind the reluctant move.

Whilst the movements of population may be seen as an essential alternative for many of communities contemporary problems, developmental or otherwise, it does not inevitably follow that the act of movement will lead to an improvement in the communities' predicaments or prospects. Like in the case of the local Kayan communities of Apoh and the indigenous people generally, land conflicts has become a major issue due to logging and large scale Oil Palm plantations that are seen as encroaching into their ancestral lands or native customary rights or NCR land.

It is indeed important to understand the different types of population movements so as to device adequate and appropriate planning and coordination strategies. Among the terms which are used in literature are three Ms: mobility, movement and migration. *Mobility* is seen as being mobile, which enables people to move from one area to another without any constraints or restrictions - the ability to afford the cost and make the necessary arrangements that facilitate the move. There is little distinction between the terms *movement* and *migration* but there are some subtle differences though. Migration is generally taken to involve the permanent or quasi-permanent relocation of an individual or group of individuals from a place of origin to a place of destination. Other forms of migration are collectively termed as *circulation* that includes *commuting* and *oscillation*. Commuting refers to movement between home and one's workplace or education, and oscillation is where people move regularly to a variety of places but always return to the place of origin.

There is also the issue of *ecologically determined movements*, especially in the more remote and ecologically marginal areas, that human activity is to a large extent controlled by nature. As Parnwell (1993) suggested, people in these marginal and remote areas have thus come to rely for their livelihood upon what nature grudgingly provides. Some of the more prevalent forms of movements includes: hunting and gathering; and shifting cultivation. *Hunter-gatherers* movements are very much a part of their way of life - associated with prevailing ecological conditions. In the old days, this is part and parcel of the way of life of the indigenous Dayak tribes of Borneo - covering vast areas of land as they track wild animals or search for wild fruits, berries and other natural produce. Today, only small remnants of the *Penan* tribe in Sarawak of Borneo are hunter-gatherers. *Shifting cultivation* represents another situation wherein people regularly move from area to area, clearing small tracts of land for cultivation. In Sarawak these are swidden farmers that practice paddy farming. These swidden farmers demonstrate a high level of dependence on nature, but characteristically live in close harmony with the natural environment. Moving from one site to another is an integral part of their balanced economic system, and because of the fragility of the ecosystem within which they operate, they cannot afford to over-exploit the natural resources upon which they depend (Parnwell, 1993).

The 'Hituk Long Atip' or 'honouring the birthplace' programmes were an eventful occasions with the total participation of the people. Various cultural activities were organized with the full involvement of the people. In the subsequent years of the 'homecoming events' the response to the programme especially in the 2000s has been a tremendous success. It is indeed encouraging that the people especially the young people are now enthusiastic and excited to go back to the village, especially at the end of each year. The better accessibility to go back is a plus factor that lures home the people. The people are now returning home regularly and frequently due to the positive impact towards the spirit of 'Hituk Long Atip'.

The underlying 'rural push factors' comes in various forces and conditions which underpin people's decisions to move to new locations. Factors such as population growth, land shortages, low level of agricultural productivity and income, and a weak non-agricultural sector have all exerted a powerful influence on the incidence of rural emigration. The selectivity of the migration process in general results in younger, better-educated, more dynamic and enterprising people move away from their home communities - a form of 'brain-drain. On the other hand, the phenomenon of return-migration mean that quite large numbers of people are coming back to their home communities, in most cases armed with improved skills, experience and perspective that a period of life and employment away from the village may have provided.

How the Kayans moved to the Baram River basin in the past was not fully understood due to the lack of documentation and evidence. Nonetheless, the migration movements of the Kayan Uma

Pu to the Apoh River valley and how they migrate from one place to another was well narrated by elders of the tribe. The Kayan Uma Pu was settled at Long Nahah'A or Batu Talang along the Baram River after the long migration pathway from Kalimantan Borneo. When the Kayan Uma Pu was at Long Nahah'A, the settlement was made up of three blocks of longhouses namely: Long Kelimau; Datah Kelawit; and Long Nyivung.

The Kayan Uma Pu of Long Atip and Long Bedian then, were found at Long Kelimau. Wan Ngau @ Taman Usung the son of Penghulu Ngau Anyie @ Nyepa, took over the Kayan Uma Pu leadership or Penghulu at the time of the emergence of the Rajah Brooke rule, which is around 1883 when the Sultan of Brunei ceded the Baram to Rajah James Brooke. Wan Ngau @ Taman Usung was instrumental in bringing the Long Atip - Long Bedian *Kayan Uma Pu* group to migrate to Apoh River valley in the early 1900s. He died at the time the group is settled at Long Belanah. This group of *Kayan Uma Pu* migrated over to Apoh River with their first settlement found at *Long Aling*, just downriver of the Melana River mouth. After some time the people moved into Melana River, and settled at the site opposite of the *Apo'* river mouth. From *Apo'* they moved down river into the main Apoh River and settled at '*Uma Ngalang*' or '*Hill longhouse*' above *Jakah lagoon*.

Nonetheless, the breakup of the *Kayan Uma Pu* started at '*Uma Ngalang*', whereby the Long Atip group under the leadership of *Emang Ngau* and *Wan Emang* moved to a site opposite of the Atip River mouth and then moved slightly upriver to a site opposite of '*Jelini Birai*' which they named '*Uma Beluveng*'. The Long Bedian group under the leadership of *Ngau Wan Taman Asung*, moved upriver and settled at *Long Map* - Map River mouth.

The British government nonetheless, wanted the *Kayan Uma Pu* to be settled together at one place. Thus, through the intermediary of Taman Tingang, the father of Baya Malang (Temenggong) under the instruction of the District Officer decided that the people settled at '*Gah Jangin*' or '*Jangin Rapids*' in Melana River. The Long Atip Kayan group built their temporary huts there with the Long Bedian group promised to go over at a later date. After the temporary huts or '*luvung*' were built, the Long Atip group set on their journey. Perhaps they may have left quite late in addition to the arduous rowing and pulling of the boats. Thus, they camped for the night at a site opposite the small *Nalin River* mouth - the present site of Long Atip longhouse which is relatively close to '*Uma Beluveng*'. However, during the night there were incessant noises of civet cats in the nearby forest that was a sign of bad omen or '*lagi*'. As a result, the journey up to '*Jangin Rapids*' was aborted, and the people returned back to '*Uma Beluveng*'. Nonetheless, they could not simply go up and enter the longhouse as the necessary rituals and spirit appeasement has to be performed. As was locally narrated: '*Nusi pah daha deng ma'un uma tua avin tekep pah na adat-adat ngioh adat lali tam Kayan*'. Thus, the migration of the Kayans of Long Atip and Long Bedian to '*Jangin Rapids*' never materialized.

The next migration of the Long Atip Kayans was to '*Uma Udik Ngalang Anak Bet*', a down river location. After a while though, the Long Atip group finally settled at the present site that kept the name Long Atip after the name of a small stream behind the longhouse which according to the calculation of Pemanca Baya Ajeng, was around the middle of the 1930s.

The Long Bedian Kayan group after settling at Long Map, moved over to Long Anyo', just above the present Long Bedian longhouse, a place they called '*Uma Tutung*' or Burnt Place' - after the great fire of the longhouse. The aftermath of the great fire compelled the people to move to a place they called '*Uma Tekayak*' the 'Encircled Village', which was presumed to be their temporary huts encircling a hill side. From there, the group moved and settled at '*Uma Ajui*' or '*Peninsula place*'. It was when they were at '*Uma Ajui*' that they were asked to join the Long Atip Kayans at '*Gah Jangin*' which never materialized. From '*Uma Ajui*', the people finally moved to Long Bedian, the present site that was also around the middle of 1930s.

The Apoh River: The landing point of Long Atip longhouse (left photo)
and the *Nalin* river mouth on the opposite side (right photo).

The people of both longhouses of Long Atip and Long Bedian are of the same stock and kinsmanship. As such, there was never any formal agreement to their area of land boundary.

Although this is the shared and common understanding, the people generally felt that there is a need to define a proper and clear boundary. Therefore, by mutual understanding and respect, it was decided that the area in the Melana River belongs to the Long Atip Kayans, and the Apoh River from the confluence of Melana River, belongs to the Long Bedian Kayans. This arrangement was mooted by virtue of river accessibility to the respective group. This understanding stands till this present day.

The land boundary with the people of Long Wat is determined by historical understanding. Thus, the boundary to the left side of Apoh River starts from *Long Tutun* from below the rubber farm of Ubung Ing (mother of Pemanca Laing Jok) moving up and going down to '*Ulat* River' at '*Long Ben'ah*', crossing '*Ulat*' River' to the ridge of *Long Win* and moving up the ridges to meet the mountain bordering Long Terawan area. On the right side, the boundary follows the '*Big Tutun* River' and then crossing and following the Tutun Lavau River, moving up the '*Pagi Ayau*' Mountain and going down crossing '*Lunang* River' and going up to the mountain top. Beyond the mountain is the '*La'ei* River' which belongs to the people of Long Bemang. Thus, the hills and mountain ridges and mountain tops tend to form the landmark and boundaries of one longhouse from another longhouse.

The scenic and nostalgic 'bird's-eye' view of Long Atip village

Arial view of Long Bedian longhouse

The Kayan translation of the boundaries of Long Atip with the neighbouring villages is as follows:

'Leka men oh aking Lung Tutun men ha'oh pulut Ubung Ing (mother of Pemanca Laing Jok) tei ma'un nesun ha' hungai Ulat ida Lung Ben'ah. Lawat Ulat tei te ji juman Lung Win tei ma'un juman tei ha Ngalang hang dahin daha Long Terawan.

Dipah aking ajui tei ma'un hungai Tutun Aya ateng hungai Tutun Lavau, mudik Tutun Lavau tei ma'un lebau ha' Ngalang Pagi Ayau. Ngileh tei nah lawat hungai Lunang, ma'un ateng ujung Ngalang. Pedah ji ngalang anan iha nah hungai La'ei, anan anun daha Long Bemang'

Arial view of Long Bemang longhouse

Population movements are interlocked with the cultural fabric of certain tribal or indigenous societies of Asia. Historically, the movements of young males from their home communities, often for several months at a time and covering long distances, represented a traditional means by which they demonstrate their bravery and prowess and their preparedness and confirmation for the transition from adolescence to manhood. Such movements as Parnwell (1993) pointed, may typically have occurred in association with tribal warfare or hunting expedition, or may have taken the form of individuals demonstrating their ability to survive, alone, in hostile territory.

The Ibans of Sarawak in Borneo have the traditional custom of *bejalai* or *'going around'*, where young men leave their longhouses to undertake journeys which may be expected to bring them material gain or social prestige. The roots of Iban *bejalai* tradition lay in the legendary tales of Iban culture heroes who experienced wild adventures during their years of wandering (Kedit, 1993; Parnwell, 1993). *Bejalai* was often closely associated with warfare and raiding including headhunting, and with trips to collect forest produce and to engage in trade. As a tradition, *bejalai* was undertaken by groups of men rather than being alone, and it is expected that young Iban men would undertake *bejalai* at least once in their lifetime (Kedit, 1993). In the present time, the Ibans have adopted the tradition of *bejalai* to include labour migration to urban centres in Sarawak and further afield (Parnwell, 1993).

The Kayans do have this culture of *bejalai* that they referred to as "*tei gaji*'" or going for 'paid employment'. The Kayans also refers to their sojourn expeditions and trips to collect forest produce like illepnuts, jelutong, resins and rattans as barter trade as '*tei kakah*' or 'going to work'. '*Tei kakah*' is the general expression of the Kayans for their daily work activities such as farming, fishing, hunting and all forms of adventures and activities that includes '*pala dau*' and other forms of free or paid labour. *Tei gaji*' or *Tei kakah* are part of the *circulation* movement or *migration* of the Kayan people.

8

The 'Sape'

The '**Sape**' (**sampet**, **sampeh**, **sapeh**) is a traditional lute of many of the Orang Ulu or "upriver people", who live in the longhouses along the rivers of Central Borneo. *Sape* are carved from a single trunk of wood, with many modern *Sape* reaching over a metre in length.

The Sape is famous among the Kayan and Kenyah tribes of Sarawak. It is used in entertainment and to accompany dances such as 'Datun Julud and 'Ngajat' - one of the warrior dances associated with headhunting celebrations in the past. Originally, *Sape* strings were made from the Sago tree that changed to nylon strings but now these have been replaced by fine steel wire and guitar string.

Initially the *Sape* was a fairly limited instrument with two strings and only three frets. Its' use was restricted to a form of ritualistic music to induce trance and tranquillity. In the last century, the *Sape* gradually became a social instrument to accompany dances or as a form of entertainment. Today, three, four or five-string instruments are used, with a range of more than three octaves.

Technically, the *Sape* is a relatively simple instrument, with one string carrying the melody and the accompanying strings as rhythmic drones. In practice, the music is quite complex, with much ornamentation and thematic variations. There are two common musical modes, one for the men's musical dance and the other for the woman's musical dance. There also is a third rarely used mode. Sape music is usually inspired by dreams and there are over 35 traditional pieces with many variations. The overall repertoire is slowly increasing. *Sape* are still being made in Borneo, and modern innovations like electric Sape are common. The varying *Sape* musical tones that are produced with the guitar and other musical instruments are a thing of concern as it will erode the authentic sound of the *Sape* in the future. There are indeed many modern versions of *Sape* musical tones that are seen as corrupting the traditional and true *Sape* music.

Who can play the most enchanting and passionate Sape music? That was the intended purpose of getting the Sape players to hone and showcase their talent during the 'Hituk Long Atip' festival in 1995.

The '*Sape*' competition begins: *Amei Ingan Madang* and the late *Amei Uvang Jok* performing their *sape* musical talent

Talented '*Sape*' players are aplenty in Long Atip.

The '*Sape*' is part of the musical culture of the Kayan tribe.

Two of the numerous great '*Sape*' players of Long Atip,
the Late *Amei Ngau Ing* (Left) and *Amei Ngau Uyo* (Right)

Amei Jok Jau and *Amei Emang Ngau* are among the great '*Sape*' players.

The great Sape players tends to create enchanting musical melody of high pitch sounds that strikes the heart of the dancer to produce a state of grandiose, a trance state of mind and body to produce a dance of grace and lightness. There is a sense of happiness and melancholy that exudes a feeling of joy that is expressed through a sense of merriment that captivates the heart and soul of the onlooker or audience.

9

Kayan Dances

Dance is indeed a very important and prominent part in the various celebrations of the Kayan tribe of Apoh Valley. Dance is the art form in which human movement becomes the medium for sensing, understanding, communicating ideas, feelings, and experiences.

Dance is a type of art that generally involves movement of the body, often rhythmic to the sound of music. It is performed in many cultures as a form of emotional expression, social interaction, or exercise, in a spiritual or performance setting, and is sometimes used to express ideas or tell a story. Dance may also be regarded as a form of non-verbal communication between humans or other animals, as in bee dances and behaviour patterns such as mating dances. Definitions of what constitutes dance can depend on social and cultural norms and aesthetic, artistic and moral sensibilities of the respective communities.

Many contemporary dance forms can be traced back to historical, traditional, ceremonial, and ethnic dance. Although dance is often accompanied by music, it can also be presented independently or provide its own accompaniment like in the case of tap dance or simply by the clapping of the hands. Dance presented with music may or may not be performed *in time* to the music depending on the style of dance. Dance performed without music is said to be *danced to* its own rhythm. For instance, beating of the gong or '*tawak*' to produce music and dance is the trademark of Long Atip village for various types of dances like 'Nyivan Sau Kayau' and 'Nyivan Upah'. Nonetheless, dances of the Kayans are always performed with the accompaniment of the '*Sape*', their very own indigenous musical instrument that is equivalent to the guitar.

Dance has certainly been an important part of ceremonies, rituals, celebrations and entertainments before the rise of the earliest human civilizations. For the Kayan tribe, dance is indeed an expression of the life and culture of the people. Various types of dances are found in the

Kayan tribe that reflects the way of life, beliefs and culture of the tribe. The type and name of each dance is reflected by the unique and specific sound from the Sape and the beat of the gongs. For instance, the sound of the Sape for the men is different from that of the women.

The various types of the Kayan traditional dances are as follows:

- '*Nyivan Lasan*' or single dance for men and women.
- '*Nyivan Sau Kayau*' or '*Tawak*' music dance.
- '*Nyivan upah*' to reflect traditional attires and lifestyle.
- '*Nyivan joh*' or long dance.
- '*Nyivan tujai*' or ladies long dance

Inei Balo Usun Ajeng gracefully performing the '*Nyivan Sin*' or solo dance.

Mr. Raymond Jok Anyie doing the difficult hand-walk and flip-flop
dance move that is performed only by an expert and great warrior

Its great fun, the '*Nyivan Joh*' or long dance is where everyone can participate

'*Sau Kayau*' warrior dance

Portraying the Kayan life style is all part of the '*Upah*' dance

The late *Amei Bui Laing Jau* is always remembered as an exemplary village elder.

Young Kayan Uma Pu basking in the merriment and celebration: Long Atip 2011

2011 Christmas Ngabang open dance performance

Inei Do' Ngau belting the '*Nyivan sin*' or single dance

Amei Jok Eng doing the 'warrior dance' with '*kelebit*' and '*parang ilang*'

Cikgu Gilbert Jau Emang performing the 'Nyivan sin'
or single dance is an excellent Kayan dancer.

The late *Amei Bui Wan Ngau* is well remembered as one of the
talented and favourite dancers of Long Atip

Unique steps and graceful swaying of the hands
creates elegance to the ladies long dance

The unique dress is part of the colourful culture of the Kayans.

The 'Hudo' dance that depicts the mysterious spirit world

The '*Upah*' dance portrays the various ways of life of the people

Performing the '*Upah*' long dance is a favourite with the people

The women folks are great dancers that showed their fine movements
and agility to match the tune of the 'tawak' music

The women folks performing the 'Sau *Kayau*' dance are great entertainers

Dancing to the tune and beatings of the '*Tawak*' and '*Sanang*'

A mix of '*Upah*' and '*Hudo Abung*' dance

The women folks performing the '*Nyivan Joh*' or the long dance

These '*hudo*' or spirits may have come from other life-forms?

'*Sau Kayau*' dances to the tune of the orchestrated beatings of the '*tawak*', and '*Sanang*'

Ngau Ing @ Taman Muring is showing the '*hudo*' or spirit warrior?

Inei Balo' Usun Emang was immersed in the fun, joy and merriment of '*Hituk Long Atip*' festival

Long Atip headman Wilson Anyie in high celebration spirit

Dance has its own content, vocabulary, skills and techniques. Dancing therefore, is made up of six elements that are expected of a dancer. As such, mastering a level of comfort and muscle memory of the first three elements is ideal before adding the other three elements. The six elements of dance are: step pattern; footwork; timing; lead and follow; style; and continuity.

The *step pattern* is the combination of steps put together to create mini sequences. These sequences can then be linked to create routines or variations. *Footwork* is the action in which we use the foot to create the technical element of the dance. For example heel, toe actions commonly used in the smooth and standard dances to create rise and fall. *Timing* is the beats of the music we move our feet to. This is to mean that the feet are being placed on the floor to compliment those specific beats. All dances have their own unique timing. *Lead* is what the gentleman is doing to maneuver the lady around the floor and through changes of direction within step patterns. *Follow* is the lady reacting to the man's lead. The lead and follow element is paramount to two people ultimately moving as one in harmony. *Style* is the element that is added to create the character of each individual dance. This can be done through hip action, arm style, body position, and movements across the floor. It can be grace and elegance that is common for many dances. Although style is like the icing on the cake to create the 'look' it is achieved by the technical elements of the first four dance elements. *Continuity* is the ability to maintain the consistency of the dance. Whether it is to link the step patterns together with ease or maintain the timing of the dance throughout the music or to be consistent with the correct footwork, we all aim to achieve that perfect dance performance. A perfect dance performance may ultimately be unrealistic but to become as consistent as possible is definitely a good feeling and will build confidence in your dancing.

The familiar cultural music of the *Sape* made the whole village of Long Atip convivial and alive.

Performing the '*Nyivan Joh*' or long dance with a mix
from the '*hudo*' or the mystic folklore faces.

Getting into the merriment and fun with all kinds of Kayan cultural artefacts

Forever in memory: The late *Inei Et Aren Ngau* leading her
group to perform the long dance or '*Nyivan joh*'.

Nyivan Tujai: A family welcoming presentation

Christmas 2011 long dance welcome performance

Young people are participating actively in the 'Nyivan Joh' or long dance

Paya Luhat belting the 'nyivan lasan' or single dance

Aren Anyie performing the 'nyivan lasan'

Sau Kayau' dance to the rhythm of the 'Tawak' sound

In the Kayan community there are many types of dances that are performed to the sound of the 'Sape' and the 'Tawaks'. Dance or 'nyivan' is part of the culture of the Kayans, but there are some in the community who are too stiff to perform it well. Dance is usually organized as part of the merriment in their numerous celebrations. The young men and women will usually get together at the veranda of the village headman to entertain visitors and guests. In the old days, dance is part of the ritual for treating and healing the sick.

An example of the Kayan dance is the 'sau kayau' a celebration dance of victory after a successful headhunting expedition. The sound and beatings of the 'gong' or 'tawak' form the music to this dance. A set of 'gongs' that includes the 'sanang', 'tuvung' and 'lutang' forms an array of instruments that creates a stimulating resonance and tempo of sounds to which the dancers leap, move, swerve and shout their heart out as a show of excitement and happiness.

'Sau kayau' dance is still performed during cultural celebrations even though headhunting is no longer practiced. The 'sau kayau' dance is an entertaining dance that can be gruelling due to a lot of running, jumping and chanting.

10

The Kayans of Long Atip

Long Atip is a Kayan village that lies in the heartland of Apoh River valley of Marudi or Baram District. Long Atip village has a dynamic and rich socio-cultural history. Long Atip was the first and only village in Apoh River to have a primary school that was established in the early 1950s.

The introduction and establishment of the Borneo Evangelical Mission was originally introduced and established in Long Atip for the Lower Baram area. Missionaries from Australia, England and New Zealand set up their base and missionary network from Long Atip. An airstrip was also built by the villagers on 'self-help' basis in the late 1950s for the missionary plane that frequented the area.

Long Atip produced the first paramount leader of the Kayans in Apoh River in the person of the Late Penghulu Anyie Ngau @ Anyi Usung @ Taman Paya Anyi who was bestowed authority by the then British colonial rule. Nevertheless, the appointment of the late Penghulu Anyi was based on the fact that he was descended from the upper class family of 'hipun uma' or 'geri uma or 'maren uma'.

The Kayans had an extremely feudal society consisting of two classes of nobles 'maren uma' one or two classes of commoners 'panyin', and slaves. The Kayans have longed practice the class or *caste* system that is still strongly and being practiced in the Kayan villages today. Status is inherited. The commoners, who are numerically dominant, were obliged to provide free labour and goods for the upper classes while the 'maren uma' were expected to manage the protection and other welfare of the community. The feudal nature of the Kayans has softened greatly in this present century together with the complete abolition of slavery and the introduction of Christianity.

Mujan Eng and the *Late Amei Bui Laing Jau* have always been cherished acquaintances in Long Atip being among the first contacts in Long Atip.

Inei Urai Wan playing the *Nose* flute or '*Selingut*' - A nose-blowing musical instrument.

Inei Ubung Eng is indeed a natural Kayan beauty with her elongated ear

This young boy was enchanted by the pomp and splendour
of the diverse and rich Kayan cultures

A Kayan beauty showing her rich Kayan culture

We want to be part of the fun, merriment and wonderful memory too

Paya Luhat wearing the *'Ta'ah'* or skirt that
was commonly worn by women in the olden days

This was a group of Kayan ladies getting ready
for their turn to perform the *'Nyivan Kayau'* or long dance

This group of young men in 'Bah' or loin cloth and women
in 'Ta'ah' were all geared for the festival

A time to remember: Get into the picture

A time to play and a time to remember

After a roaring performance: A time to store it into the memory

One for the album: Group Two Troupe Members

Group Three Troupe Members

Part of Group Two Troupe Members

The young men and ladies were passionately involved in the cultural dance

Amei Jok Jau is one of the highly respected elders
donned in full Kayan warrior attire

Nawan Luhat donning the great Kayan warrior headgear '*Lavung*', holding the '*kelebit*' or shield and wearing the '*sunung*' getting ready to perform the '*Nyivan Sin*'

Jok Emang in full Kayan warrior costume ready for his '*Nyivan sin*'

The rope pulling 'tug of war' was the climax of the Telematch 1995.

Feeding time for the 'babies' contest 1997

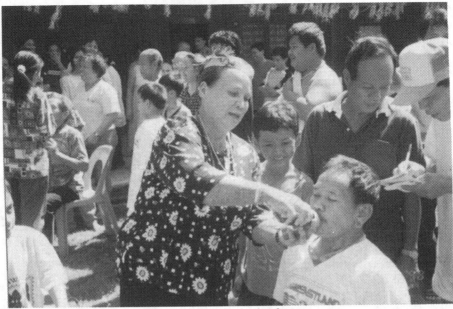

Which baby feeds the fastest?

In the past, travelling to the longhouses in Apoh was by means of river transport. The journey takes between 5 to 6 hours from the town of Marudi to Long Bemang, 8 hours to Long Atip and about 9 hours to reach the furthest longhouse of Long Bedian. Travelling to these villages was very arduous and tiring using the longboat powered by a 20 to 40 horsepower outboard engine.

The opening up of the hinterland of the Apoh valley to timber or logging activities facilitate the construction of timber roads from Temala Camp along The main Baram River to the interior of Apoh. These timber roads nonetheless, pass further away from the longhouses. Towards the end of the 1980s, the villagers sought the cooperation and help of these timber companies to build access road to the longhouses. Thus, an access road of around 16 kilometres was built to Long Atip around 1985, as part of their corporate social responsibility.

To get to the longhouse of Long Atip, one has to cross the Apoh River. In those early days, a long boat has to be used to cross over. Imagine the unloading and loading of goods one has to bring to the longhouse. In 1987 a suspension bridge was built under the Agriculture Community Development programme to connect the longhouse to the other side of the river. In 2011, a more permanent Bailey bridge was built across the Apoh River to replace the suspension bridge. The bridge was indeed built at the most opportune time because after one week of completion and using the bridge, the suspension bridge suddenly and naturally collapsed into the river. Thus, a tragedy and calamity was avoided at the right time that was attributed to divine help, providence and intervention.

Prior to the implementation of the Bailey bridge the people of Long Atip have to use a suspension bridge. To get to the longhouse, one has to physically shoulder all articles and materials which was an arduous task for everyone. With the completion of the Bailey bridge, driving directly to the village is indeed a marvellous experience. The people can now drive their vehicles right to their doorsteps which was a far cry from those early years of 2000 and beyond. Life has indeed changed for the better for the people, at least in terms of accessibility and convenience. The people are however, looking forward to better road condition from the existing dirt-road to tar-sealed road as the country progresses.

To get to Long Atip village, one has to cross this suspension bridge

The suspension bridge crossing Apoh River leading to Long Atip village is now history

River landing point: The use of longboat has been a major means
of transport in Apoh River in the past.

Village jetty Long Bedian

River landing point during low tide: Long Atip village 2013

The Bailey bridge crossing the Apoh River at Long Atip
On the right is the suspension bridge

Long Atip Bailey Bridge built in 2011

The timber road can be very slippery, muddy, dusty and extremely risky

Access road to Long Atip is slippery earth road that is very dangerous to motorists

Accessibility to the rural villages of Apoh River valley is mostly by land through tough logging roads. In the past, river is the only means of transport to the rural villages in Apoh River. With the opening of the rural areas to logging activities in the 1970s, land transport has become an alternative mode of travelling and accessibility to the rural villages in Apoh River. Nowadays though, river transport is rarely used by the people to return back to their villages.

The choice of land transport is the better alternative to villages in Apoh River and to the rural areas in Baram today. However, the roads are actively used by the logging industry which makes it extremely dangerous to use and to travel. Furthermore, the logging roads have their peculiar rule of use for driving a vehicle. Thus, one has to be very alert and familiar with the directions that are being put up along the roads, and one has to either drive on the right or left of the road as is indicated by the signage put up along the road.

Driving along logging roads will have to be on the right as indicated by the signage

The access roads to the villages of Long Bemang, Long Wat, Long Atip and Long Bedian are dirt or earth roads that are very slippery and dangerous during the rainy days. As these roads are the only alternative mean of travel nowadays, the government should come up with a rolling development plan to gravel and tar-seal these roads. Furthermore, there is no consistent maintenance of the roads and the people have to rely on the goodwill of the logging companies to maintain the roads as and when requested.

Waiting for YB Datuk Patinggi Tan Sri Alfred Jabu on a visit to Long Atip

A crowd of Long Atip villagers preparing to 'Lalu'
or welcome YB Datuk Patinggi Tan Sri Alfred Jabu.

Welcome to Long Atip YB Datuk Patinggi Tan Sri Alfred Jabu. 23rd December 1998.

Welcome dance for YB Datuk Patinggi Tan Sri Alfred Jabu.

Christmas party: Long Atip 2011

Break time during the concreting of new extension of Long Atip church on 14.10.2013

The participation of the people in the '*Nyivan upah*' was so overwhelming

Doing the '*Nyivan upah*' depicting a hunter on a hunting trip

The ladies '*Nyivan joh*' or long dance was indeed the crowd puller

The young girls did not want to miss the fun too.

The warrior kids were trained from young about their unique culture.

The thrill and melancholy of the '*Nyivan joh*' was there to savour.

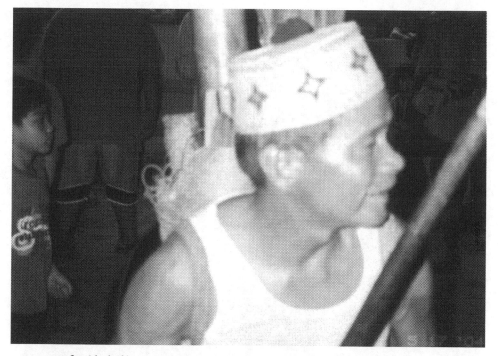

A farmer going for '*kakah*' or working in his farm? This was all part of the dance performance.

The unique head band of the ladies participating in the 'Nyivan upah'

The rich cultural artefacts of the Kayans were indeed magnificent.

This was a 30 strong-member '*Nyivan upah*' led
by the great warrior *Amei Ingan Madang*.

This young hunter is going after the squirrels that disturb his fruit farm.

The Kayan '*Hung*' or umbrella embroidered in beadwork.

Reminiscing the past creates a nostalgic moment to the older folks.

These young girls have the natural inclination to step into the legacy of the past.

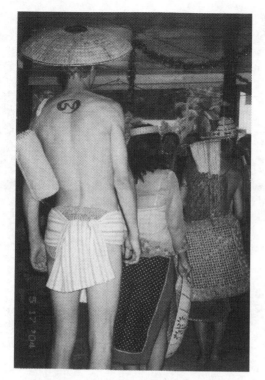

This young tourist was fascinated with all the thrills and stepping
in line with an impromptu loin-cloth wear.

These young men were going to 'Kakah' or work to set their fish trap.

Beautiful and colourful young maidens in unique traditional attires

The Kayans are indeed rich in traditional and cultural artefacts

Amei Anyie Ajeng is leading his pack of warriors for the 'Warrior dance'.

'Nyivan upah' by group or gang two members

Aren Nawan is naturally talented in performing the Kayan *'Nyivan joh'*.

Nathalie and Aren are indeed proud of being part of the dance group.

This warrior was on his way to hunt wild boar?

The 'Nyivan upah' group or gang one members

These young ladies were dressed in full traditional dress.

A group of men on their way to the farm for '*pala dau*'

Nawan Luhat ready to go to the farm?

The '*Nyivan upah*' is always a thrill.

After the 'Nyivan upah' - A time to cherish for a life time

Et Ubung Jok @ Hinan Aren Anyie performing the 'Nyivan Lasan'

11

'Pagen' or the Resting Platform

The **'Pagen'** which is found at Long Atip portrays an interesting and intricate legacy about the *Kayan Uma Pu* of Apoh River. Nonetheless, what is so unique and intriguing about this *'Pagen'*? *'Pagen'* in the Kayan language is a resting platform or sitting table which is slightly raised about 25 centimetres above the floor.

The 'Pagen' measures 240.4 cm by 170.2 cm of the buttress root of a Tapang Tree

The 'Pagen' is a gift of profound gratitude from the people of Long Bemang

The '*Pagen*' is found at the veranda of the house of the late Penghulu Tama Paya Anyie, the former Paramount Chief of the *Kayan Uma Pu* of Baram District. The Kayan Uma Pu of Long Bemang moved from Batu Talang or Naha' A in the 1940s at the behest and advice of Penghulu Tama Paya Anyie, whose group moved over to Apoh River in the 1930s. His concern and pity on the *Kayan Uma Pu* that were left in Batu Talang compelled him to coax and convince the people to move to Apoh River. Perhaps the importance of being in one area is also a significant factor as well.

Migrating from one place to another is a mammoth and arduous task indeed. When the group finally moved to Apoh River, they have to row or paddle their boats down the Baram River and moving up the Tutoh River and the Apoh River. When they reach the mouth of Apoh River, their kinsmen from Long Atip were there to receive them, and from there they travelled up together to Long Bemang where they were asked to settle. As a show of gratitude and appreciation to Penghulu Tama Paya Anyie, the people presented the '*Pagen*' to the Penghulu.

The '*Pagen*' measures 240.4 centimetres long (8 feet) and 170.2 centimetres (5 feet 7 inches) wide. It is cut from the huge buttress of a Tapang Tree found in the Bemang River valley. The Tapang tree must have been huge to accommodate such a large buttress root. The buttress is cut and hewn by sheer hard work and physical strength using the axe or '*Kapak*'. The fine spirit of kinsmanship and cooperation has made it possible to execute the various tasks successfully and easily under the context of teamwork through the principle of: '*berat sama dipikul, ringan sama dijinjing*'.

Imagine how the men push and pull it through the jungle? To lift it up requires many strong and sturdy men as much as possible. To carry it in the thick jungle with the deep terrain and hills is beyond one's imagination. It was told that the '*Pagen*' was transported on two longboats tied side by side and rowed and pull up the Apoh River from Long Bemang to Long Atip. At that time there was no outboard engine. Thus, the men have to use oars and poles to row and push the boats. As such, the value of the '*Pagen*' is indeed priceless which is full of meaning, purpose and importance. The '*Pagen*' indeed, represents the loyalty, unity and solidarity of the *Kayan Uma Pu* towards their '*Maren Uma*'.

Koompassia excelsa, also known as Tapang, or **Mengaris**, is an emergent tropical rainforest tree species in the *Fabaceae* family. It is known by different names in different regions - *Mengaris* in Brunei and Sabah, *Tualang* in Peninsular Malaysia, *Sialang* in Indonesia, and *Tapang* in Sarawak. In the Kayan dialect it is called '*Tanyit*' and '*Tanid*' in Kelabit. The name Tualang comes from the Malay words of *tua* - old, and *helang* - eagle. The *Koompassia excelsa* tree is among the tallest tropical tree species in the world, and also one of the most prominent trees in the tropical rainforests. The tallest measured specimen is 85.8 metres or 88 metres (281 or 289 ft) tall. The tree is found in Sumatra, Borneo, South Thailand, and Peninsular Malaysia. The grey, whitish bark of the tree, large bole and often handsome crown makes it usually stand out amongst the other trees.

Tapang or '*Tanyit*' grow mostly in lowland rainforests where they tower over the canopy. Like most tall rainforest trees it has huge buttress roots to support its weight. This is also because the majority of the nutrients in rainforest soil are very near the surface, making large spreading roots more effective than deep ones.

The *Tapang* tree is revered by the indigenous people of Sarawak. There is a taboo in Sarawak against cutting down the *Tapang* tree. Only naturally felled Tapang trees (usually by an unusual storm or a landside which might be natural or even unnatural) can be used. Furthermore the Dayaks do not cut their Tapang tree in their temuda or farm because it is a valuable source of honey and a home for the Great Kenyalang or Hornbill. Hornbills on the other hand control the snake population in Sarawak and Borneo.

The indigenous tribes use the wood in a very discreet way as they continue to respect their traditional taboo against cutting Tapang trees. . A small piece may be cut off from the buttress root which will not kill the tree, for the handle of a parang or axe or as the pestle for their mortar. Tapang wood is hard to cut by an ordinary cleaver or sword. A special axe called the *Beliung or Kapak* is used. Nonetheless, the task is very labourious, arduous and physically taxing. Thus, we can rightly say that it is not really an honest thing to accuse the local farmers of destroying the forest of Sarawak. For instance, Tapang trees nowadays are usually felled by bulldozers or chainsaws as the tree is very hard and tough.

The tree starts to have branches only from 30 meters upwards. The silvery and slippery tree trunk is a remarkable natural protection for the tree. Only the best tree climbers can harvest the honey from the Tapang trees.

Most of the Tapang trees have been felled recklessly by logging operations without kind regard to the spirituality of this particularly tree. According to local beliefs men who used chainsaw to fell the Tapang would have their own retribution - a son may die or the family fortune wiped out. Hence with this naturalistic belief tied to the environment the ancestors of the Dayaks were natural environmentalists who were at peace and respectful of Mother Nature.

If anyone ever come to Long Atip, make it a point to view and examine this great gift and token by the *Kayan Uma Pu* of Long Bemang to the late Penghulu Tama Paya Anyie who made it possible for the people to migrate from Batu Talang or Naha' a, to the Apoh River and settled at Long Bemang.

The Pagen of Long Atip

A Tapang Tree is easily recognized. The buttress is usually huge to support the trunk

This 'Pagen' is estimated to be 70 years old. The surface has become
very smooth naturally after years of use, wear and tear.

12

'Pah Lung' or feasting together

'*Pah lung*', feasting or eating together is a traditional culture amongst the natives of Sarawak. This unique get-together is a party where everyone in the village works and cooperates to prepare food and drinks either for lunch or dinner for the whole village. For a big village of about 115 doors like Long Atip, a tremendous effort of preparing food requires selfless contribution and cooperation of the people.

The time to serve the folks during the '*pah lung*' or eating together for the whole village 1995.

'Pah lung' is a unique culture of the Kayans of Long Atip 1997.

'Pah Lung' or eating together at the longhouse basketball court 1997

Eating together along the longhouse veranda was enjoyable 2005.

'*Pah Lung*' or eating together for fun and sharing of food 2009

Christmas Pah Lung Long Atip 2009

'Pah Lung' Long Atip longhouse 2011

'*Pah Lung*' Long Atip longhouse 2011

'*Pah lung*' is indeed a great way to share and taste the various and sometimes exotic foods of the Kayans. Each family will prepare their own choice of foods and then bring it together to the common veranda of the longhouse to be shared with other people. So this is a kind of pot bless that is commonly practised amongst the indigenous tribes. This has become a culture amongst the *Kayan Uma Pu* of Long Atip. Additional and extra foods like chickens or pork and drinks are usually provided by the Village Development and Security Committee for the occasion.

'*Pah lung*' creates an atmosphere of merriment and conviviality. It is a time to share common stories and update each other about current and personal affairs or just to catch up with each other in an informal way and atmosphere.

13

Pagan Tawak: Beating of the Gong

A gong Indonesian: *gong*; Malay: *Canang*, or *Tawak* in Kayan is a type of flat bell percussion sonorous or musical instrument of Chinese origin and manufacture, made in the form of a broad thin disc with a deep rim, that has spread to Southeast Asia.

Gongs vary in diameter from about 20 to 40 inches, and they are made of bronze containing a maximum of 22 parts of tin to 78 of copper; but in many cases the proportion of tin is considerably less. Such an alloy, when cast and allowed to cool slowly, is excessively brittle, but it can be tempered and annealed in a peculiar manner. If suddenly cooled from a cherry-red heat, the alloy becomes so soft that it can be hammered and worked on the lathe, and afterwards it may be hardened by re-heating and cooling it slowly. In these properties it will be observed, the alloy behaves in a manner exactly opposite to steel, and the Chinese avail themselves of the known peculiarities for preparing the thin sheets of which gongs are made.

In the old days, the use of the 'Tawak' was very restricted to important events and happenings. In fact, the beating of the gong or 'Tawak' tends to create apprehension, anxiety, doubts and fear amongst the people. The beating of the "Tawak" though is an emergency call to gather the people together immediately. This is reflected in the manner of the beating and the sound of the 'Tawak'. For instance, faster and incessant beats reflects urgency for the people to gather themselves together. A slow, soft and longer interval of beating of the 'Tawak' tells of the passing of a person in the longhouse. Thus, the 'Tawak' was used to inform the people of the passing or death of a person in the village. The '*Tawak*' is also used to search for people who are lost on a hunting trip in the jungle. The '*Tawak*' is beaten consistently that will help to attract them to the search party. To get a wider coverage of the sound of the '*Tawak*', the search party will have to climb the top of a mountain and hills to beat the gong.

The 'Tawak' is an instrument of music to the Kayans of Apoh, and particularly to the Kayans of Long Atip. The beating of the gong or '*Pagan Tawak*' has become a rhythmic sound that is synonymous to Long Atip longhouse. The most enchanting, melodious and entertaining *Pagan Tawak* in Sarawak is found in Long Atip. '*Pagan Tawak*' has become a central musical sound for Long Atip longhouse. '*Pagan Tawak*' is made more attractive and unique with the *Nyivan upah* and *Nyivan Sau Kayau* or the fleeting dance. The dancers will dance, fly and float to the sound of the *Tawak*. Several sets of the '*Tawak*' are used to provide a melancholy of distinct and individual sound of each gong or '*Tawak*'.

The flair and energy of 'Nyivan upah' came from the music of the 'Tawaks'.

The beating of the 'Sanang' and 'gong' contributed to the thrilling merriment of sounds.

The bigger 'Tawak' is a must to the whole spectrum of music and dance.

A gong is an ancient musical instrument that originated in Asia. The origins of the gong have been traced as far back as 2000 B.C. However, it is believed that the gong was used long before this time. The gong was important to the people of Asia, and this continues to be so today. In the past, owning a gong was a sign of wealth. To the Kayans, owning a gong or '*Tawak*' is a priceless possession. It denotes one's authority, status and wealth in the community. Thus, it is not common for a commoner to own a 'Tawak'. Marriages of the *Kayan Maren Uma* use the '*Tawak*' for the married couple to sit on. Gongs are perceived to have positive effects on its owner such as; its power of positive energy could bring good fortune; and the power could be obtained simply by touching it.

Southend High School UK students playing the 'Tawaks' during their stay at Long Atip from 18.7.2013 till 22.7.2013 under the World Challenge programme

Cikgu Mering Ibau (now a Penghulu) participating in the '*Upah*' long dance

Village warriors performing the '*Sau Kayau*' dance

A mixture of men and women getting ready to perform the 'Sau Kayau' dance

Dancing to the *Pagan Tawak*: These women folks were always the crowd puller.

These women were recollecting their dress wear of the past?

This woman is going to '*Nyikap*' fish in the small stream near the village.

Paya Luhat is performing the '*Nyivan upah*' to the beat of the 'tawak'.

These wonderful ladies performing the '*Nyivan upah*' to the sound of the '*tawak*' music

Long Atip women folks 'Pagan Tawak'

A complete set of Tawaks owned by Long Atip village

14

Melodious songs of '*Nak na*' and Badi

The famous Kayan song is the singing or chanting called '*Nak na*'. The '*Nak na*' is sung by a lady or man with the melodious accompaniment of a group of men and women at intervals or at the end of each sentence. The '*Nak na*' is sung in the form of extortion or poem or '*Leken*' of welcome, praises and appreciation to honourable guests that visit the longhouse or during celebrations to honour the elders that have contributed greatly to the development and betterment of the village. To sing the '*Nak na*' is indeed a talent as not every man or woman can recite the '*Leken*' in the '*Nak na*'. In Long Atip very few people can sing the '*Nak na*'. One of the famous and well known '*Tekna*' singers is *Usun Wan* or commonly called *Hinan Jalong Liwan*. Her exceptionally high pitch and strong melodious voice is very captivating, enchanting and buoyant to the listeners.

Singing the '*Nak na*' as '*peleken*' to honourable guests led by Hinan Jalong.

Saying the '*Nak na*' requires melodious accompaniment of ladies and men.

A group of ladies gathering together to sing the '*Nak na*'

The ladies saying the '*badi*' which is part of the Kayan oral chanting

Chanting the '*badi*' makes for a joyful merry-go round dance

Dancing the '*Nyivan joh*' in consonance with the chanting of the '*liling*' song

The '*liling*' provides the melody for the graceful '*Nyivan joh*'

These ladies are wearing the '*Lavung lunuk*' or head band.

These ladies and young girls were preparing to join the '*Nyivan joh*'.

An example of 'Leken' in 'Nekna' as sung and recited by the Penans of Long Buang is included to show the meanings in a 'Leken' as well as how it is expressed:

The headman *Melai Bali* has the natural talent and knowledge of the Penan ancestral songs. He dedicated his 'Leken' to us for visiting his longhouse.

TK Melai Bali, Long Buang

"First, He apologized for the simple welcome accorded as this was all they could afford to organize. He nonetheless, thanked us for the trouble and time to stop at his village. This shows that the government is caring and very concern for the Penan community. Not many government people stop by their village in recent times. He hoped that the 'orang pelitah' will come to their village more often to teach and help them to improve their livelihood. He reiterated that the government has always treated the Penans with special care and attention.

They are always confident that the government will continue to give them more development. They want to follow and support the government. The government determines their future. He hoped that the government will continue to teach them better ways to improve their lives. They are faced with many challenges. Their farms are not productive due to attack by insects and sparrows. The wild boar, deer and birds of the jungle are gone. The jungles do not provide them their food anymore. Therefore, they need the government to teach and give them better ways to grow crops and livestock. Education of their children is very much dear to their heart. Somehow they are often faced with the problem of 'tidak ada belanja'. Thus, they are unable to keep their children in school. They hope to be more successful in getting their children to school in future. For health, they are very thankful to the government in giving them water supply. They are no longer worried about having to take bath or get their water supply from the muddy Apoh River anymore. Their health is much better when compared to our ancestors. We hope that the government will continue to teach us more ways to have better health. We are very happy with the government for taking care of our health. We wished all the visitors a safe journey back. May you all have good, successful and long life! Don't forget us as you go back to Kuching and Marudi. All the best, till we meet again".

Atan Apun and Rudang Bangan

Another two older ladies *Atan Apun* and *Rudang Bangan* also sang their '*Nak* na' and '*Leken*' to us. "We are indeed very happy to have you '*pelitah*' visiting our old simple longhouse. We welcome you with all our heart. We have nothing to offer you. We look forward to the government to make better house for us. We are poor and cannot build better houses. You can see for yourself how we live. Take pity on us. We know the government can do a lot of good things for us. We live very hard and difficult lives. We are '*sutuk*' because we are not good in '*manu kerja tong tana*' or toiling the land. We feel ashamed in showing our weaknesses. But we just have no choice. We want you '*pelitah*' to take care of our future. We want better life like you people in town. You give and open the opportunities and ways for us to be like you people. We pray for better life and success to you people so that you can continue to help us. You remember us when you go back. '*Ketelu' pelitah jian mu'un*', you government people are always good. Thank you, thank you".

15

Tattooing or *'Nedek'*, wear, Beadworks, and 'Penghut'

The Kayan people are very colourful people that are reminiscent of their rich culture, beliefs, and their close association with their natural environment. Their costume and nature of dress are very much reflected by their values and their way of life. The traditional headwear, *'Teba'ang'*, elongated ear, and sash with typical *'Ikeng'* design are all part of the Kayan identity. Hose (1926) pointed that the Kayans are the most and best tattooed tribe in Borneo in the old days, and it is to them that most of the other tribes owe their knowledge of tattoo and the majority of the designs. Tattoo or *'Tedek'* is part of the Kayan culture and identity. The Kayans are particularly fond of tattooing with the women more so than the man. A Kayan woman is tattooed in complicated serial designs on the upper part of the hands and over the whole of each forearm; on both thighs to below the knees, and on the upper part of the feet and toes. The pattern is so close that at a slight distance, the tattooing appears simply as a mass of dark blue, and the designs, some of which are very pretty, usually consist of a multiplicity rings and circles. And those of the higher status or rank have in addition one or more small spots on the breasts.

According to Hose (1926), the start of the making of *'Tedek'* begins when girls are about eight or ten years of age, at first the hands and feet, and afterwards, prior to arriving to the age of puberty, the other parts are finished. The tattooing of a Kayan girl is a serious undertaking, not only because of the pain and inconvenience caused but also on account of the elaborate ceremonial requirements. The process is a long one, lasting three to four years as only a small piece can be done at a sitting and several long intervals elapse between the various stages of the work. The girl when about ten years old has probably had her fingers and feet tattooed, and about a year later her forearms should be completed. The thighs are partially tattooed during the next year, and in the third or fourth year from the commencement of the whole operation are thus completed. It is considered immodest to be tattooed after motherhood.

The design of a '*Tedek*' is first carved on a wood that projected out. It is then smeared with the sooty preparation and printed on the skin. The figure is then punctured in outline with a set of needles dipped in ink, and afterwards the whole figure is filled up in detail. More ink is poured on to the skin and allowed to dry into it. Rice is smeared over the inflamed skin to keep it cool. If this is not done, the skin is apt to gather and fester. The limb or area operated upon must be kept from being wet, and must not be scratched however much it may itch.

Tattooing or '*Nedek*' process is done by dipping a pricker into the pigment, taps its handle gently with the striker, driving the needle points into the skin at each tap. In tattooing or '*Nedek*' the performer pricks the design or pattern with three needles, and afterwards smokes it with a dammon torch, by which process a beautiful dark blue mark is produced. Frequently inflammation of a serious nature follows. There is no antiseptic precaution taken and a newly tattooed part often festers, but looking at the tattoos done, one is bewildered by the fact that tattoos are very seldom spoilt by scars.

For one to undergo tattooing or '*Nedek*' has to endure an excruciatingly painful experience. The subject can rarely restrain her cries of anguish. One has to be held firmly, cajoled, encouraged, or even rebuked when undergoing the tattooing. This is so because, the girl will cry, shout, and plead for the tattooing to be stopped. But the tattooist is unmoved and proceeds methodically with her task. For a young girl of *Maren Uma*, the process of tattooing is somehow mandatory. The accomplishment of having tattoos though, is a cherished dream of any young lady in the Kayan community. Tattoo or '*Tedek*' is an important element that shows the strength, courage and beauty of a Kayan maiden. This is indeed a way of attracting or showing oneself to any young man or a prospective husband.

In the old days the class restriction with regard to tattoo was very strict. The more intricate and elaborate tattoo is reflected on the status of the girl, especially the *Maren Uma*. Thus it is always possible to distinguish between the daughters of the '*Maren Uma*' and those of the ordinary common-woman and dependents, by the finesse and number of the lines composing the patterns. The designs for the lower-class women are not nearly as complex as those of the '*Maren Uma*', and they are generally tattooed free-hand. Among Kayan women tattooing is universal. They believed that the design act as torches in the next world and that without these to light them would make them forever in total darkness. They also believed that after death the completely tattooed women will be allowed to bathe in the mythical '*Telang Julan*' river and that consequently they will be able to pick up any precious articles and stones that are found on the river bed. The incompletely tattooed women can only stand on the river bank, whilst the untattooed ones are totally not allowed to approach its banks.

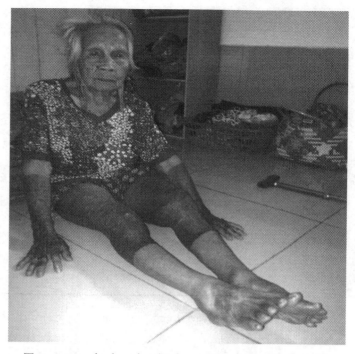

Tattoos on the hands, thighs and feet of a Kayan lady

The tattooed hands of a Kayan Lady making 'Selukung' of glutinous rice

Kayan Ladies showing their tattooed hands and elongated ear of
'*Iseng Sabau*' for the lady on the left.

Mujan Eng showing off her attractive elongated ear and tattooed hands
that was the pride of Kayan maidens in the old days.

Among the Kayans tattooing is always done by a woman, and the position of a tattooist is to a certain extent hereditary. In the old days tattooists are believed to be under the protection of a guardianship spirit, who must be appeased with sacrifices before each process of tattooing or '*Nedek*'. The greater the number of sacrifices offered or the greater the skill and experience of the artist, the higher the fee demanded.

The tools used by a tattoo artist are very basic, consisting of two or three prickers and an iron striker that are stored in a wooden box. The pricker is a wooden rod with a short pointed head fastened at right angles at one end. The point of the head is attached a lump of wax in which are embedded three or four short needles - their points alone projecting. The striker is merely a short iron rod, half of which is covered with a string lashing (Hose, 1926; Roth, 1968). The pigment used for the colour is a mixture of soot, water or sugar-cane juice, and it is kept in a double shallow cup of wood. It is supposed that the best soot is obtained from the bottom of a metal cooking-pot, but soot derived from burning resin or 'damar' is also used. The designs are curved in high relief on blocks of wood, which are smeared with the ink and then carefully pressed on the part of the body to be tattooed, leaving a clear impression of the designs.

How the tattoo artists get paid is more or less fixed. For the fingers, the tattooist is paid a '*malat*' or short sword. For the forearms a gong or '*tawak*' worth from eight to twenty dollars is required. In the Baram River though, a gong can only be demanded by an artist of about twenty years experience, and lesser-known artists have to be contented with beads and cloth. For the thighs a large brass '*tawak*' or big gong worth from six to sixty dollars according to workmanship is warranted (Hose, 1926). The fees may be paid in instalments, but before the knee cap, the last part to be tattooed, is touched, the artist must be paid the full amount. Where the subject is unable to pay the artist accordingly, she has to pay the equivalent in the form of physical labour which is referred to as 'mebet dau tedek' that may happen amongst the lower-class women folks.

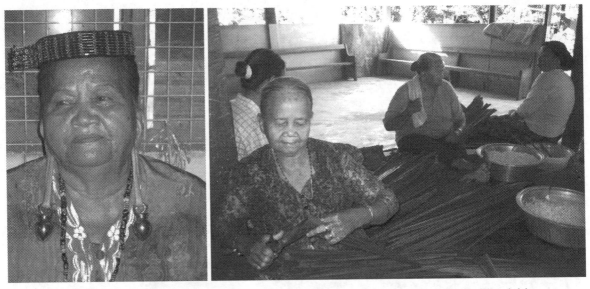

The uniqueness of a Kayan woman: The headgear, elongated ear-lobe and 'Tedek'.

The Kayan ladies are always having their unique indigenous fashion

The uniqueness of a Kayan woman: Usun Eng with her 'Tedek' and beads wear

Kayan Ladies of Long Atip in their full traditional and colourful dress

Inei Unyang Wan wearing the '*Lavung lunuk*'

Inei Devung Ajeng with her elongated ear and brass *'Iseng Sabau'*

Cliff Emang Jau wearing a traditional Kayan headwear adorned during celebrations and festivities.

A Kayan Lady donning the Kayan traditional headwear,
'*Teba'ang*, elongated ear, and sash with typical '*Ikeng*' design

A **bead** is a small, decorative object of various shapes and sizes, being solid or hollow, but usually pierced for threading or stringing. Beads range in size from under 1 millimetre to over 1 centimetre in diameter. Beadwork is the art or craft of making things with beads. Beads can be woven together with specialized thread, strung onto thread or soft, flexible wire, or adhered to a surface such as fabric or clay. The oldest-surviving synthetic materials used for bead making have generally been ceramics: pottery and glass.

Precious beads and fine beads

Small colourful, fusible ceramic beads can be strung into necklaces or bracelets, or woven into key chains. Fusible beads come in many colors and degrees of transparency or opacity, including varieties that glow in the dark or have internal glitter; peg boards come in various shapes and several geometric patterns.

Most glass beads are pressed glass, mass-produced by preparing a molten batch of glass of the desired color and pouring it into molds to form the desired shape. This is also true of most plastic and ceramic beads. Modern mass-produced beads are generally shaped by carving or casting, depending on the material and desired effect. In some cases, more specialized metalworking or glass-working techniques may be employed, or a combination of multiple techniques and materials

Ceramic beads are made by taking various colors of clay and rolling them out into pencil-thickness lengths. They are then packed together, side by side, to form a much thicker length of clay, with the colors arranging a desired pattern. The clay mass is once again rolled out thin so each color comprises a smaller but longer portion of the mass. Cut the clay lengthwise into bead-width pieces. A hole is poked through the centre of the bead and its edges are either rounded or flattened. With the shape and color complete, the beads are then fed en masse into a kiln to be baked hard. A finishing layer of glaze gives them a shine.

Beads can be made from most and any decorative material. Thousands of plastic beads are made at a single time by filling empty molds with colored liquid plastic and then allowed to dry. They may also be made from many types of metal, both precious and common, by the same process. Beads from precious metals are more often made by hand as this adds to their uniqueness and worth. Beads can also be made from hand-worked stone such as jade, obsidian, and jasper. Their color, shine and individual grain of the stone make each of them a treasure.

Kayan precious and ornamental beads

The indigenous tribes and more so the Kayans, see beads as supernaturally attractive. Beads are frequently used in ritual offerings in the old days, and wear them during important ceremonies. In the early times, beads are a symbol of wealth. 'Good' beads are not only very valuable, they also reflect on the status in the community. There are numerous types of valuable beads or *'Inu pa'un'* in the Kayan community. *'Inu Pa'un'* is original beads that have been passed as heirlooms through the generations that have become priceless. The various priceless beads of the Kayans and the Orang Ulu generally are: *Lukut Sekala'* (Bela); *Lukut Selibau*; *Matan Tiung Paun*; *Pelangalan*; *Kelampuyo' Pa'un*; *Tubē Ata'*; and *Lavang*. The *Lukut Sekala'* is the most priceless of all the beads of the Kayan tribe. The ownership of such beads in the old days is accurately known throughout a large district which is equivalent to the ownership of masterpiece of ancient art in modern time. The wife of a chief or headman may possess old beads worth thousands of dollars, and wear a large part of them on any occasion of feasts and celebrations.

Various kinds of 'Inu Pa'un

'Inu Pa'un' old beads that are seen as priceless by the Kayans

Old beads as mentioned earlier are very much valued and sought after by all tribes but especially so by the Kayans. There are few families of the upper class or *'maren uma'* that do not possess a certain number of them while the richer women often have what must be quite valuable collections. At one time indeed, they seem to have been used as currency. Many varieties are well known, and some of the Kayan women are very expert in recognizing the genuine old beads, and in distinguishing these varieties from one another and from modern imitations.

Necklaces of precious old beads

Beads are adorned on all creation of beauty and colours of the Kayan life. Beads are worn as ornaments of beauty that adds glamour and colour to the wearer. Indeed the wearing of beads creates the charms, splendour and attractiveness to the wearer - young or old. The heavy ornamental wear of the indigenous tribes throughout the world exudes an opulence of art, beauty and natural creativity of the communities. In the Kayan tribe, one can see it on the dress, native hats or '*Hong*', baby carriers or '*Avat*', sword-sheaths, head-bands, cigarette-boxes and all forms of Kayan artworks that reflects on some animistic or spirit forms which are reminiscent of the past tradition, cultures and beliefs of the Kayans. The colours of the beads are selected according to the demands of the pattern over which they are used.

The beads are worn threaded together to form necklaces and girdles, being arranged with some reference to harmony of size and colour and add value, the most valuable being placed in the middle, where they can be shown to best advantage and position. A woman who possesses a good collection of such beads will seldom be seen without some of them on her body. She will generally be eager to add to her collection. And she may occasionally make a present of one or two beads to some highly honourable friend or relative and will generally divide them, but without handing them over, to various female relatives before her death.

Fine beads as artworks of the Kayans

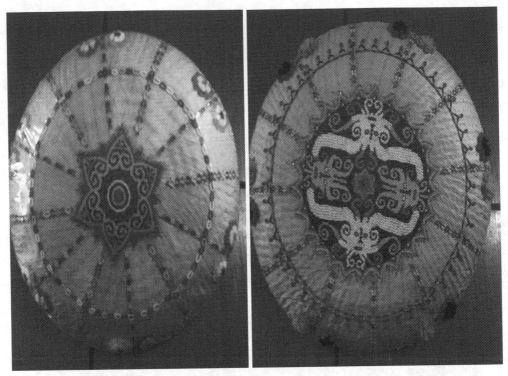

Fine beads threaded together as decorations on the 'Hong' or native hats

The design or 'Ikang' reflects the animistic belief of a 'spirit face'

Typical '*Ikang*' that reflects the spirits and animistic beliefs of the past

'***Penghut***': This is the fine and thin strands of wood that is sliced carefully as a decorative item. It is the natural way of creating and putting up decorations by the Orang Ulus, and more so by the Kayan Uma Pu of the Apoh River.

'*Penghut*' is prepared for significant events as a form of decoration that is synonymous with the indigenous tribes of Sarawak. It reflects the symbol of naturalness, uniqueness, and attractiveness that portrays the life and closeness of the natives to its natural environment.

'*Penghut*' is made from fine, tough soft wood of the jungle. Young trees are normally selected to make the '*penghut*'. The 'penghut' is the authentic and classic decoration that is commonly seen during important events that reflects the identity of the people, especially those from the Kayan-Kenyah tribes.

Doing the 'penghut' requires an expert hand.
The expert showing the art and skill in making the 'penghut'

Making the 'penghut' requires concentration, deft hand and a very sharp knife.

'Penghut' the Indigenous tribes decorations for ceremonial occasions

Making 'penghut' appears easy but the demonstrations proved that the task requires an 'old hand' to make good and elaborate 'penghut'.

16

Cooperation: 'Hadui Peji' or Self-help spirit of the Kayans

Community action in the context of the indigenous tribes of Sarawak works on the basis of community cooperation and participation. Community participation revolves around pooling together scattered resources both material and human and channel these resources through teamwork. This form of contribution can be examined from cooperation in behavioural theory (Axelrod, 1984). From the community perspective, cooperation involves a symbiotic and symmetrical social relations based on mutual trust without any vested interest, which is related to reciprocity. A strong foundation of reciprocal behaviour is tied to culture. Reciprocity works on the basis of "do unto others as you would have them do unto you" kind of philosophy. As Axelrod, (1984) emphasized, "strong reciprocators possess two behavioural dispositions: they are willing to bestow benefits on those who have bestowed benefits, and they are willing to punish those who fail to bestow benefits according to social norm." This implies that reciprocity becomes a prerequisite to achieving symbiotic interdependence among group members as social collectivity. On the other hand, cooperation between local actors and outside agents, say in this case, government agents, tends to carry a contrasting meaning. As far as the state's agenda are concerned, cooperation requires local community to pledge loyalty to a third party for supporting the latter.

Community participation can also be drawn into the perspective of the 'tragedy of the commons' dilemma model (Hardin, 1968). Self-interested individuals are unlikely to capture joint benefits, unless people who share the commons collectively work together. The commons can be viewed as public good. Hellwig (2003) argues that "the more people share the cost of public good the less the individual participant has to contribute." Therefore, in a vast range of situations mutual cooperation can be better for both sides than mutual defection. If this is the case, according to Tuomela (2000), cooperation is also grounded in social behaviour as kin-altruism and reciprocal altruism. As

Hogg (1992) reiterated, cohesiveness traditionally seems to mean 'bonded, mutually attracted, and cemented', which cause a range of measurable group behaviours such as attitudes, performance, amount of communication, discussion directed at changing the opinions of dissidents, conflicts, acceptance or rejecting of individuals as members, and the adoption of common standards.

The uniqueness of the Kayans is found in their spirit of kinsmanship, self-help and cohesiveness. These have evolved into their culture of '*hadui peji*' or self-help spirit in all spheres of mutual help that affect or relates to community work and activities. These has been built and strengthened through the feudal system of the past. During the start of the paddy farming season, the people will meet to discuss the '*hadui peji*' to '*mahap*' to the village headman. '*Mahap*' is the culture of launching the start of paddy season whereby the villagers will converge together to clear the land for the village headman to begin the farming season. The first day of activity has to be done to the village headman before the others in the village can commence their own farming. '*Mahap*' was done for the village headman for all aspects of paddy farming from clearing the land, to burning, planting, weeding, and harvesting of the paddy. '*Mahap*' is no longer practiced but the other forms of community self-help spirit are still practiced in the Kayans of Apoh River today.

The Kayans both men and women, are hardworking people. The work of paddy planting for instance is divided between the men and women. The men clear the jungle and prepare the land. In planting the grain the men folk walk along and by means of a long pointed pole make holes about one foot apart for the reception of the seeds. The women follow behind and drop a few grains of paddy into each hole.

'*Hadui peji*' is seen in the daily life of the Kayan people. The people just love to work together. The men and women folks will give their whole hearted spirit to '*hadui peji*'. When the people have a feast celebration, the men and women will go and give a helping hand. The men will bring their '*malat*' or machete and '*i'yuh*' or knife to butcher, cut, and cook and slice the meat. The women folks will be busy in the kitchen cooking the '*Selukung*', pancakes and vegetables, and wrapping the cooked rice in e type of broad leaf, the '*daun isip*'.

In the old days during an occasion of marriage or celebration before dawn, a man will call out or '*muvui*' along the length of the longhouse hallway for the men of the whole longhouse to rise up to work together or '*nyadui peji*'. The men will come along with their tools, equipments, materials and other items that they can contribute or use in their special way for the work to be done. As was narrated:

'Nei nah daha' lake' geri angan, taring lajang, seh kayo' tayun, iuh, dahin malat. Putung-putung la'ung nyadui ngioh haman dahin deng ji-ji la'ung atih. Daha' aleng geri taring lajang na kanen. Balei nevek dahin puyah uting dahin maru na' lim. Hu'uh

sak uting nei nah balei lake' geri iuh dahin malat, ngayan ti'au halem haruk aleng hu'uh mayau ma'ang ngavan na hadui anan'.

'Every men will turn up bringing along their working knives, short sword, cooking pot stand and cooking pot, bundle of firewood, and start to do their work according to the tools and equipment they brought - based on their individual skill and ability. Those that came along with their cooking items will start to cook the rice. Some others will proceed to slaughter and dress the pigs meant for the occasion. When the meat is cooked, some men will come along to slice the meat in a longboat that has been washed and cleaned for the task'.

Everyone is working tirelessly on the task that they are prepared and focus upon, in the spirit of kinship, unity and self-help that is inherent in the Kayans of Apoh Region. The spirit of self-help is basically a culture of the indigenous tribes in Sarawak and much so amongst the Kayans of Apoh. This culture is imbued in the community due to the bond of cohesiveness and kinsmanship brought about by their leaders or Maren Uma of the past that is still preserved and relevant till this present day. It is indeed important to maintain and uphold this legacy so as to maintain the spirit of togetherness and bond of Kayan Uma Pu for the betterment, progress and well-being of the community into the future.

Men folks taking time while cooking rice for a celebration

The veranda is the common place for self-help work

Women folks wrapping the cooked rice for a celebration

Women folks frying the '*dinuh*' a Kayan pancake delicacy

The women will do their part of packing the rice or '*napai kanen*', frying the 'dinuh' and make the 'selukung' that are their indigenous delicacy and identity. The occasion is very interacting, jovial and convivial-like.

Preparing and frying the indigenous 'dinuh' or pancake of glutinous rice

Women '*nyadui peji*' to wrap their rice in leaves on the longhouse veranda

Men preparing the cooked meat for a wedding celebration in a longboat

The men folks butchering the pig for a feast celebration

The men folks are cooking the rice in big pots

The women folks are a major force in community based activities

Women folks helping to wrap up the cooked rice

In life we are always up against the challenges of trying to find strength in unity, but that cannot be found when there are so many differences and so diverse a membership. Thus, the important thing is not to let the differences get in the way of cooperation. We have to be tolerant, sympathetic and sincere toward each other.

'*Hadui peji*' refers generally to the context of *community participation*. Community participation can be loosely defined as the involvement of people in a community in projects to solve their own problems. Nonetheless, people cannot be forced to 'participate' in projects which affect their lives but should be given the opportunity where possible. This is held to be a basic human right and a fundamental principle of democracy. Community participation is especially important for programmes and activities that provide mutual benefits and interests, as well as in emergencies and disasters. Community participation though, can take place during any of the following activities:

- **Needs assessment** - expressing opinions about desirable improvements, prioritising goals and negotiating with agencies.
- **Planning** - formulating objectives, setting goals, criticizing plans.
- **Mobilizing** - raising awareness in a community about needs, establishing or supporting organizational structures within the community.
- **Training** - participating in formal and informal training activities to enhance communication, construction, maintenance and financial management skills.
- **Implementing** - engaging in management activities; contributing directly to construction, operation and maintenance with labour and materials; contributing cash towards costs, paying of services or membership fees of community organizations.
- **Monitoring and evaluation** - participating in the appraisal of work done, recognizing improvements that can be made and redefining needs.

Nevertheless, we have to be aware of the fact that many community programmes tend to be designed and executed by the lead agency; and, this does not mean that the community is unable or unwilling to participate in some or all of the activities as outlined above.

However, the following are some of the main reasons why people are usually willing to participate in community or humanitarian programmes:

- Community participation motivates people to work together - people feel a sense of being a community and recognize the benefits of their involvement.
- Social, religious or traditional obligations for mutual help.

- Genuine community participation - people see a genuine opportunity to better their own lives and for the community as a whole.
- Remuneration

There are often strong genuine reasons why people wish to participate in programmes. All too often government aid workers assume that people will only do anything for remuneration and have no genuine concern for their own predicament or that of the community as a whole. This is often the result of the actions of the agency itself, in throwing money or food at the community members without meaningful dialogue or consultation. Remuneration is an acceptable incentive but is usually not the only, or even the primary motivation. In the *Kayan Uma Pu* clan, community participation is a natural way of life that is rooted in their culture of mutual help for their common good.

In *the Kayan Uma Pu* there is no gender bias in community programmes

Another significant aspect in community work is *community mobilization*. Community mobilization applies to the way in which people can be encouraged and motivated to participate in programme activities. In order to mobilize a community successfully it is important to identify where people's priorities lie and what it is that motivates them. A useful starting point is to identify community leaders in order to establish key contacts between the agency and the community. Care must be taken in doing this to ensure that all community members are represented.

It is important to remember that no community is completely homogenous but is likely to be made up of people of wide range of backgrounds and characteristics. Therefore, what motivates one group of people within a community may not motivate others. A strong religious belief may motivate some people to participate, whilst the opportunity to raise one's status or position in society may be a much stronger motivating force for other community members. Capacity building at community level on the one hand, may be important to develop skills and build confidence. For instance, this may be especially important for women who may lack experience of contributing to community planning. Capacity building through skills training and confidence building can be a key ingredient in mobilizing different sections of a community.

17

Kayan Names

What's in a name? The sweetest sound to the ear, to the person and to the soul is the call of one's name. Nonetheless, what is there in a name?

Freud and Shakespeare both recognized that the relationship between name and identity is so strong that the misrepresentation of a name amounts to a misrepresentation of the person (Smith, 1967). The sense of personal identity and uniqueness that a name gives us is at the heart of why names interest us and why they are important to us as individuals and to our society as a whole. In spite of their importance, though, most people know very little about names and about the effects they have on us and on our children in daily life. In a very real sense, we are the users of names, and as such, we have the need and right to know about the psychological, magical, legal, religious, and ethical aspects of our names (Feldman, 1959).

To those who are well acquainted and familiar with the indigenous tribes of Borneo, and Sarawak in particular, the name of a person is significant as a way to recognize and differentiate his or her ethnic or racial identity. This is indeed very true to the Kayans of the Apoh River valley where the name will provide an instant recognition of their ethnicity - except for a few names that are common with their distant sub-group, the Kenyahs. Nevertheless, they are differentiated further by their distinct physical features and appearance. The various indigenous tribes of Sarawak though will be able to recognize their particular racial ethnicity through the name of the person.

For the Kayans, they are easily recognized by their names. The names amongst the Kayans are unique as it revolves around certain and limited names that are exclusive to their tribe. Thus, there will be hundreds of Kayans with the same name. The names of the Kayans are as Per Table below. As such, there will be hundreds of Kayan men with the name Anyie Ajeng, Anyie Wan, Anyie Ngau, Anyie Jok, Anyie Eng and so forth. The same goes for the name Jok Wan, Jok Jau,

Jok Ngau, Jok Eng, and similarly for the name Jau are: Jau Jok, Jau Wan, Jau Ngau, Jau Eng etc. For the name starting with Wan are: Wan Jok, Wan Jau, Wan Ngau, Wan Eng and so forth. The name of the individual however, have to be associated with the longhouse or village they come from or by the name of their first born son or daughter, such as Taman Emang Wan or Taman Paya Luhat - '*Taman*' means father of Emang Wan or father of Paya Luhat.

A name may seem like a small matter, but it really is not. When you are on a first-time meeting with people, you should be saying and spelling their names correctly. It is not funny, and neither is it proper to brush aside a person's name as if it is not important. For the women, their names will evolve around their father's name. For instance, for the name Aren, there will be many similarities in the name such as: Aren Anyie, Aren, Jau, Aren Jok, Aren Emang, Aren Ding, Aren Nawan and so forth.

Table: Kayan common names for men

Anyie	Jalong	Lah	Pahang
Ajeng	Jok	Laing	Paren
Avit	Juman	Lawai	Tingang
Balan	Kajan	Luhat	Usung
Ding	Kalang	Manuk	Uvang
Emang	Kawit	Mering	Uyo
Ibau	Kelawing	Nawan	Wan
Jau	Kilah	Ngau	

Table: Kayan common names for women

Aren	Idang	Mujan	Ubung
Bungan	Iring	Pagang	Uding
Bulan	Lahei	Paya	Ulau
Do'	Lahung	Ping	Unyang
Devung	Livan	Puyang	Usun
Dau	Long	Tening	Uyang
Hunai	Lunai	Tipung	

In this modern time though, the people tend to adopt English names for their children. Some parents nevertheless, still include an indigenous middle name to their children to maintain their identity. However, the original tribal names will continue to be diluted and corrupted that will endanger the future identity of the indigenous tribes such as the Kayan Uma Pu of Apoh River. Hopefully, the future generations of Kayans, Kelabits, Kenyahs and other '*Orang Ulus*' will be proud to call themselves by their particular tribe and race through the preservation of their indigenous names.

In the past the Kayans have names given to a man and woman who's first born child or any other child has died. These sympathetic names or '*aran pasi*' are given to show sympathy or pity to the family. When a first-born child has passed away, the name '*Bui*' will be given in addition to the name of the man. For instance, if the first-born child of Wan Jok died, he will be called by the name '*Bui* Wan Jok' thereafter. For any other child that has died, the man will have the word '*Akem*' added to his name as '*Akem* Wan Jok'. If both a boy and girl have died in a family, the name '*Uyung*' will be added to the name - '*Uyung* Wan Jok'. For a man whose wife has died, he will have the name '*Aban*' added to his name.

The woman folks also have their '*aran pasi*' as well. When a first-born child has died, the name '*Uyu*' will be added to the name - '*Uyu* Aren Jau'. If any other child has died, then the name '*Et*' will be added to the name - '*Et* Aren Jau'. For a woman who has lost her husband, she will have the name '*Balo*" added to her name - *Balo'* Aren Jau.

18

Education the way forward

A Chinese proverb says: "If you are planning for a year, sow rice, if you are planning for a decade, plant trees, if you are planning for a lifetime, educate people". Education is indeed one's passport to betterment and productivity in life. Education that is translated into skills and knowledge and embodied in an individual is basically defined as human capital. A person can attain a certain stock of human capital and this is primarily influenced by education and training. It is generally argued that investment in human capital increases productivity. The work of Adam Smith through his classical growth model and human capital model suggested that an educated worker is likened to an expensive machine. The skills embodied in a person can be "rented out" to an employer. As Florides (2003) pointed out, the higher the level of skill a person has the higher the "rent" is likely to be. Thus, the expected returns on investment in human capital are a higher level of earnings and greater job satisfaction over one's working lifetime.

As the World Bank emphasizes, education opens doors and empowers. For people, it opens up a world of opportunities, reduces the burden of disease and poverty, and gives greater voice in society. For nations, it opens doors to economic and social prosperity, spurred by a dynamic workforce and well-informed citizens that are able to compete and cooperate amongst themselves in the world at large. Workers produce not just by using their muscles and physical might, but primarily by using the wide variety of skills embodied in the human mind.

Education is the key to success. Education is a good indicator that reflects an achievement of courage and perseverance. The achievement of the highest possible tertiary education is the pride of the individual and family members. Generally, education is the life-line to a better livelihood for the individual and the family. There are many arguments and debate about education, nonetheless, the reality in this modern age is the fact that education is indeed the passport to one's better future and success. The crucial entry point to one's betterment in life lies in one's educational attainment and success. Through education, knowledge is built which is the foundation and secret of success in this borderless world. As emphasized by Armstrong (1995), Stoner et al (1995), Daft (2000), Bloom et al 1956), Stantrock (2011), Woolfolk (2010), the importance of education creates numerous benefits as follows:

- Better knowledge and understanding
- Produce better confidence and self-esteem
- Accord respect and dignity
- Create better capability and ability to perform one's work
- Higher preference for employment
- Higher remuneration and income
- Continuous stimulation and effort for greater improvement and betterment
- Greater ability for creativity and innovation
- Better capability for analytical and critical thinking
- Greater capability and capacity for leadership and managerial function and performance
- Continuous pursuits for professionalism, excellence and quality.

Looking at the development of education amongst the Kayans of the Apoh valley, it seems to follow simultaneously with the advent of Christianity to the people. With the acceptance of Christianity by the people of Long Atip, education was initiated by the missionaries as well. The young men and adults of the longhouse were taught the alphabets, and how to read and write. The intention of the missionaries then was to enable the local people to read the Bible and sing songs of worship. The immediate and long term intention was to get the local villagers to lead in worship and share the word of God. Thus, the development of church deacons and elders was established for each village or longhouse.

The coming of the missionaries was indeed an added blessing for the introduction of education amongst the Kayans of Apoh. Perhaps greater benefit then was to the people of Long Atip where the first formal school to educate the Kayans of Apoh that started at the village by the beginning of 1950. The young men and girls of the villages of Long Bemang, Long Wat, and Long Bedian have to go over to Long Atip to pursue their upper primary education of standard five and standard six. Some of these young men were already matured and strong adults that helped tremendously the younger ones. Imagine these young people that have to paddle up or down to Long Atip just to get an education.

One needs the grit and exceptional determination to succeed in one's education then. Paddling up from Long Bemang will take up a full day compared to the three hours boat ride powered by an outboard engine, presently. Thus, the strong and determined young people will survive these tough conditions in addition to the standard four and standard six examinations that they have to pass. Any student who fails these examinations will mean that they are not able to further their studies. Therefore, the elimination process for a good and better education was very challenging experience in those old days of schooling.

One of the success stories of education amongst the Kayans of Apoh is in the person of **William Anyie Jok**. He is one of the pioneers in going to school in Apoh as well as a pioneer in bringing education to the Kayans of Apoh River and for Baram generally. William Anyie Jok @ Taman Vivian Anyie is a pioneer amongst the Kayans of Baram to have become an educationist for the betterment of the community. His 34 years of teaching and educating the young Kayan children has been illustrious, colourful and memorable. Indeed there were also numerous challenges, problems, difficulties and sacrifices that went with these memorable experiences.

Life has been good to this man as a young boy in his pursuit for better education. The opportune and material time of the arrival of the Christian missionaries to this remote and inaccessible place in Borneo, opened the door for education to *William Anyie Jok*. As the missionaries established their Mission Centre at Long Atip, the setting up of the first school for the young people started in the early 1950s. William has been very fortunate to be amongst the pioneer students of this mission school. On the top of that, Long Atip School was amongst the pioneer schools established in Apoh

River valley, and perhaps among the pioneer schools in Baram beside Bukit Sabun School Long Lama.

According to *William Anyie*, he was indeed fortunate in his initial primary school years. The missionary, who manage the Mission Centre, Pendita *Ubung @ Leah Cubit*, has a soft spot and compassion for this young boy. This Pendita paid a close and personal attention to him in his daily school work. And this has imbued and instilled a deep sense of commitment, dedication and responsibility in him in his later life as a successful teacher. The fine Christian teaching and the finesse touch of a thorough breed English lady has had a profound effect that shaped his life towards total commitment and dedication to his 34 years teaching profession and endeavours.

William went for his teacher training at Batu Lintang Teachers College from 1967 to 1968. After completing his training, his first posting as a trained teacher was at his home-place of Long Atip from 1968 to 1969. His subsequent postings were as per Table below.

Table: William Anyie teaching career postings

School	Year
SK Long Bedian	1970 - 1978
SK Long Atip	1979 - 1984
SK Benawa	1985 - 1986
SK Long Tungan	1987
SK Long Atip	1988 - 1997
SK Long Bemang	1998
SK Ubung Emang	1999

William retired from the teaching profession in December 1999. Looking back into his teaching career, his most satisfying and happy moments were the success of getting his most outstanding students to obtain Yayasan scholarships in furthering their studies into secondary-level education. His personal effort and recommendations has enabled these poor rural students to further their studies. A total of five students, three from SK Benawa and two from SK Long Tungan, obtained these scholarships. During his second posting back to Long Atip, the school obtained the Best Primary Six Examination results for three consecutive years, and even surpassed the national average for one year. He was given the privilege to brief the school teachers in Baram about his experience in managing his school to achieve excellence. Many headmasters adopted his programme that made their schools successful as well. His tenure at SK Benawa has made the school to achieve the Best Boarding School award for Miri Division.

Long Atip has produced the most number of teachers in Apoh. Some of the early educators from Long Atip were Gilbert Jau Emang, Jok Emang, Cliff Emang Jau, Frederick Uyo Jau, Lajim Jau, Martha Luhat and many others. Nonetheless, there are many other professionals found in Long Atip. And the most number of graduates in Apoh valley are from Long Atip. The summary record of graduates from Long Atip longhouse is as per Table below (Gabriel Ding, 2006).

Table: Record of graduates from Long Atip longhouse

Academic Qualification	Number
Masters Degree	12
Bachelor Degree	70
Diploma	72

Source: Records from Mr. Gabriel Ding Jau (2006)

It is indeed pertinent and important that the Kayan community at large should appreciate the values, concepts and various literatures pertaining to education as discussed hereafter. Education benefits society in many ways. More educated workers tend to have lower unemployment rates and received higher wages. Therefore, society benefits by receiving more taxes. Florides (2003) opined that more poorly educated workers may also find crime an attractive means of supplementing their lower incomes. Society may benefit from investing in education by paying less for social welfare programmes and crime prevention. The children of more educated parents tend to received better guidance and grow up in a more desirable environment.

Blaug (1972) argued that if the social rate of return exceeds the private rate of return then more investment in human capital should take place. Social rate of return also provides us with the rationale that education should be subsidized with public funds. McConnell and Brue (1989) are of the opinion that, the size of these public subsidies to education should be determined on the basis of the magnitude of the associated social benefits. Nonetheless, the social rate of returns is very favourable. Therefore, based on the arguments of Blaug (1972) and McConnell & Brue (1989), the governments of LDCs should subsidize education. This is also argued on the basis that, a majority of the populations is in the low-income and poverty groups. As is widely known, education is the key to promote growth and alleviate poverty, and it fair enough that the government have to provide the welfare cost.

The importance and development in education is seen in many perspectives. For instance, "education is seen as empowering people to take charge of their lives and make informed choices. It fosters equity and social cohesion by providing people with access to productive assets such as land and capital, and by increasing labour mobility and earning potential. An additional year of schooling raises incomes by 10 percent on average and by much more in low-income countries.

Education builds nationally competitive economies by helping a country to develop a skilled, productive labour force and to create, apply and spread new ideas and technologies. It promotes good health by encouraging children to practice healthy behaviours and avoid risky ones; giving youths the knowledge and values to avoid contracting diseases such as HIV/AIDS; and empowering women to have few children and better care for themselves and their family. Education though, gives voice to the disadvantaged and is fundamental to constructing democratic societies" (World Bank, 2003).

Malaysia has consistently placed a high priority on the need for good and sound education and training, be it academic or vocational (Najib, 1995). The government has invested heavily on the human capital and will continue to do so into the future. The private sectors have also followed the government in investing on human capital. This will benefit not only their requirements but will also benefit the creation of a greater and larger pool of human capital. The government recognizes the reliability of human capital compared to physical capital. History has shown that when a country places too much emphasis on physical capital and neglect human capital, it has been unable to sustain growth. Nonetheless, practical concerns have to be considered about the financing of education. As Spencer (2003) emphasized, public education cannot be provided entirely free if financial viability of the educational sectors is to be maintained. Education, important as it is though, is only one of a multitude of factors influencing the level of human capital (Florides, 2003).

The Education Blueprint of the nation is to produce quality individuals through the practise of high-level thinking, be fluent in English and have a strong sense of ethics. Students will be poised to make waves in the world job market as the Education blueprint aims to expand their potential and produce global leaders. As such, if we have to compete on the global stage, we must ensure that we meet international standards for our education system. The Malaysian Qualification Framework (MQF) emphasizes on eight domains of learning outcomes as follows:

o   Knowledge
o   Practical skills
o   Social skills and responsibilities
o   Values, attitudes and professionalism
o   Communication, leadership and team skills

o Problem-solving and scientific skills
o Information management and lifelong learning skills, and
o Managerial and entrepreneurial skills

This requires students to go beyond rote memorization skills of surface approaches and develop deeper research and analytical and critical thinking skills, to think out of the box creatively and be able to make a better tomorrow for our society at large.

Learning can be defined formally as the act, process, or experience of gaining knowledge or skills. In contrast, memory can be defined as the capacity of storing, retrieving, and acting on that knowledge. As Santrock (2011) emphasized, learning as a relatively permanent influence on behaviour, knowledge and thinking skills that comes about through experience. It includes observable activity and internal processes such as thinking, attitudes and emotions. Learning helps us move from novices to experts and allow us to gain new knowledge and abilities. Learning strengthens the brain by building new pathways and increasing connections that we can rely on when we want to learn more. Definitions that are more complex add words such as comprehension and mastery through experience or study (Woolfolk, 2010). Physiologically, learning is the formation of cell assemblies and phase sequences. Children learn by building these assemblies and sequences. Adults spend more time making new arrangements than forming new sequences. Our experience and background allow us to learn new concepts.

At the neurological level, any established knowledge (from experience and background) appears to be made up of exceedingly intricate arrangements of cell materials, electrical charges, and chemical elements. Learning requires energy; re-learning and un-learning requires even more. We must access higher brain functions to generate the much-needed energy and unbind the old (Santrock, 2011).

Remarkably, people can learn from the moment of birth. Learning can and should be a lifelong process. Learning shouldn't be defined by what happened early in life, only at school. We constantly make sense of our experiences and consistently search for meaning. In essence, we continue to learn (Steinbach, 1993). Though humans like the familiar and are often uncomfortable with change, the brain searches for and respond to novelty. Rote learning frustrates us because the brain resists meaningless stimuli. When we invoke the brain's natural capacity to integrate information, however, we can assimilate boundless amount of information.

In today's business environment, finding better ways to learn will propel organizations forward. Strong minds fuel strong organizations. We must capitalize on our natural styles and then build systems to satisfy needs. Only through an individual learning process can we re-create our environments and ourselves (Woolfolk, 2010).

Critical thinking is the intellectually disciplined process of actively and skilfully conceptualizing, applying, analyzing, synthesizing, and/or evaluating information gathered from, or generated by, observation, experience, reflection, reasoning, or communication, as a guide to belief and action. In its exemplary form, it is based on universal intellectual values that transcend subject matter divisions: clarity, accuracy, precision, consistency, relevance, sound evidence, good reasons, depth, breadth, and fairness.

Critical thinking as postulated by Scriven & Paul (1987) can be seen as having two components: (1) a set of information and belief generating and processing skills, and (2) the habit, based on intellectual commitment, of using those skills to guide behaviour. It is thus to be contrasted with: (1) the mere acquisition and retention of information alone, because it involves a particular way in which information is sought and treated; (2) the mere possession of a set of skills, because it involves the continual use of them; and (3) the mere use of those skills "as an exercise" without acceptance of their results. Critical thinking varies according to the motivation underlying it. When grounded in selfish motives, it is often manifested in the skilful manipulation of ideas in service of one's own, or one's groups', vested interest. As such it is typically intellectually flawed, however pragmatically successful it might be. When grounded in fair-mindedness and intellectual integrity, it is typically of a higher order intellectually, though subject to the charge of "idealism" by those habituated to its selfish use.

Critical thinking of any kind is never universal in any individual; everyone is subject to episodes of undisciplined or irrational thought. Its quality is therefore typically a matter of degree and dependent on, among other things, the quality and depth of experience in a given domain of thinking or with respect to a particular class of questions. No one is a critical thinker through and through, but only to certain a degree, with confined insights and blind spots, subject to selected tendencies towards self-delusion. For this reason, the development of critical thinking skills and dispositions is a life-long endeavour.

Everyone thinks; it is our nature to do so. But much of our thinking is biased, distorted, partial, uninformed or down-right prejudiced. Yet the quality of our life and that of what we produce, make, or build depends precisely on the quality of our thought. Shoddy thinking is costly, both in money and in quality of life. Excellence in thought, however, must be systematically cultivated.

Critical thinking is that mode of thinking - about any subject, content, or problem - in which the thinker improves the quality of his or her thinking by skilfully taking charge of the structures inherent in thinking and imposing intellectual standards upon them.

As Santrock (2011) emphasized, some ways teachers can consciously build critical thinking into their lesson plans are:

- Ask not only what happened but also 'how' and 'why'.
- Examine supposed 'facts' to determine whether there is evidence to support them.
- Argue in a reasoned way rather than through emotions.
- Recognize that there is sometimes more than one good answer or explanations.
- Compare various answers to a question and judge which the best answer is really.
- Evaluate and possibly question what other people say rather than immediately accept it as the truth.
- Ask questions and speculate beyond what we already know to create new ideas and new information.

Bloom's taxonomy shows and reflects on the development and evolution of critical thinking in a student. Bloom, et al (1956), Bloom (1994), reiterated that the taxonomy begins by defining knowledge as the remembering of previously learned material. Knowledge represents the lowest level of learning outcomes in the cognitive domain. Knowledge is followed by comprehension, the ability to grasp the meaning of material and goes just beyond the knowledge level. Comprehension is the lowest level of understanding. Application is the next area in the hierarchy and refers to the ability to use learned material in new and concrete principles and theories. Application requires a higher level of understanding than comprehension on the part of a learner.

In analysis, the next area of the taxonomy, the learning outcomes require the student an understanding of both the content and the structural form of material. Next is synthesis, which refers to the ability to put parts together to form a new whole. Learning outcomes at this level stress creative behaviours with a major emphasis on the formulation of new patterns or structures. The last level of the taxonomy is evaluation. Evaluation is concerned with the ability to judge the value of material for a given purpose. The judgments are to be based on definite criteria. Learning outcomes in this area are the highest in the cognitive hierarchy because they incorporate or contain elements of knowledge, comprehension, application, analysis, and synthesis. In addition, they contain conscious value judgments based on clearly defined criteria. The activity of inventing encourages the four highest levels of learning-application, analysis, synthesis, and evaluation--in addition to knowledge and comprehension to a learner or student (Bloom, 1994).

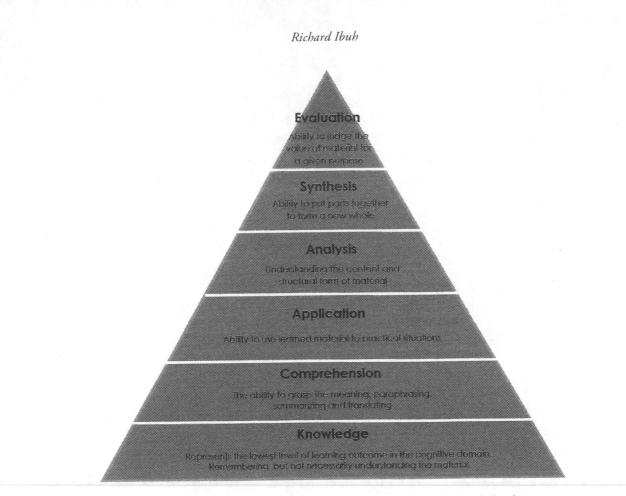

Figure: Diagrammatic drawing of Bloom's Taxonomy of critical thinking.

Academic excellence nonetheless, is not sufficient for success as other qualities such as character, high moral and discipline of mutual respect are equally essential to form a well-refined individual. In life though, if you can imagine it, you can achieve it. If you can dream it, you can become it. Nonetheless, life has always been challenging, ambiguous and unpredictable and more often held back because of the fact that our yesterday has been coloured by our past; but our tomorrow can actually be coloured by our own choice.

19

Kayan Marriage

Marriages amongst the Orang Ulu and particularly amongst the Kayans have been influenced by their Christian belief, the urban nature of lifestyle and the changing social values amongst the younger generation. Most marriages nowadays are also mostly held in the towns and cities. Thus, church marriage tends to be the preferred choice of the affected couples.

Nonetheless, traditional weddings have become a part of the Kayan marriages which is fervently advocated by the Kayan leaders such as the Paramount Chief of the Orang Ulu Temenggong Pahang Ding. The need to rediscover the traditional form of Kayan marriage is indeed a commendable effort of the Kayan community as a way to revive the Kayan marriage tradition and culture. Thus, a mix of church and traditional Kayan marriage is of profound importance especially to the *Maren Uma*.

The traditional wedding process and associated rituals vary in accordance with the respective social class of the man and of the woman to be married, and of their respective families and longhouses within the Kayan community. The present day class structures and hierarchies are the outcome of centuries of events and occurrences amongst the Kayans such as warfare, enslavement, voluntary social associations, arranged marital unions, and various traditions spanning over many generations. This aspect of Kayan culture has turned out to be crucial in terms of determining the nature as well as the ritual form of marital unions that is: who can or cannot marry who, what wedding procedure is to be followed, and who is allowed to perform what ritual.

In the typical traditional Kayan wedding, prior agreement is made by the couple's family the items to be given as *jai* to be given to the respective parents and siblings that commensurate with the family status. The *jai* is done at the wedding. For instance, the jai given by the groom's parent to the bride's parents is in the form of *tawak*. Jai *tawak* is not considered as exchange or barter but more of a symbol that the man is now taking care of the daughter. The tawak is to be kept by the bride's parents in their original *amin* or house. The siblings are given the *malat buk* or *malat* or *parang ilang* according to the class structure. Normally, the men are given the *parang ilang* and the women are given the sarongs. The panyin is expected to give *agung* as jai to the bride's parents.

Kayan Paramount Chief Temenggong Pahang Ding
expounding on the Maren Uma marriage.

Village Chief performing the traditional Maren Uma marriage ritual

VIP photo call at a Maren Uma marriage ceremony celebration

Traditional marriage: Undergoing the marriage ritual

A village Chief conducting the traditional Maren Uma marriage

Maren Uma marriage: Shielding the newly married couple

In the traditional Maren Uma wedding, there are eight men and eight women accompanying the bride and the groom. The couple is seated on the tawak with the woman sitting on the left of the groom. The groom has the shield held above the head to provide protection. For the bride, hornbill-feathers decorated hat or *hong* is held over her head as protection. The others will hold similar hat but without feathers. For the *Maren Uk*, there are four men and four women accompanying the bride and groom. For a panyin wedding, the couple will be seated on a decorated wooden bench or *ladong* with one attendant. Commoners cannot sit on the *tawak* during their wedding as the tawak is associated with the status of aristocracy.

Church marriage is an integral part of Kayan *Uma Pu* marriage practice

Family album: A church wedding ceremony at Canada Hill Church in Miri

In the old days, the mode of courtship amongst the indigenous tribes that includes the Kayans is quite peculiar. No courting goes by the day, but at night, when all is quiet a young lover creeps to the side of the curtain or net of his lady-love and awakes her. The girl normally sleeps apart from their parents, more often in the loft. The nocturnal visiting or '*ngedoh*' goes on for some weeks.

This nocturnal visit goes on for some weeks. If the parents of the girl think the match a suitable one, the young pair is permitted to see each other very often and more openly. On the one hand, if the young man does not find favour with the parents of the girl, they soon will let him know that his visits are not welcomed. They do not allow their daughter to see him alone, and the matter ends naturally. The night courtship or '*ngedoh*' though, is the only way for the man and woman to become acquainted with each other, for such a thing as privacy during the day is quite uncommon in the Kayan village.

When the young couple have decided on their future to their mutual satisfaction, the next step is for the man to make known his wishes to his parents who then make arrangements for their relatives and friends to meet the girl's parents to request formally the hand of their daughter in marriage. This consent is seldom refused because as a tradition the parents of the girl approve of her choice, otherwise they would not have allowed the man to '*ngedoh*' their daughter.

There is usually a great deal of discussion, sometimes lasting for days, as to where the married couple are to live after being married. The wife does not always '*ngivan*' or leaves her home to go and live with her husband. As often as not the man takes up his abode in the house of his wife's family. Many matters are taken into consideration in deciding where they are to live. If the daughter is the only child, the parents generally make it a condition of the marriage that the son-in law should come and live with them, and work for them, but where the girl has many brothers and sisters, and the man has not, she is allowed to go and live with the husband. Nonetheless, the question of social status needs to be considered, and if the girl marries a man of lower rank the family expects the man to come to live with them. When everything has been satisfactorily arranged, and the consent of the girl's parents has been obtained, a day is fixed for the marriage ceremony.

The wedding may take place either at the house of the bride, or else at that of the bridegroom. Generally, it is held in the house in which the newly married couple do not intend to reside. For instance, if it has been decided that the newly married wife should settle in her husband's house, then the wedding will take place at her home. If, on the other hand the relatives decide that the husband is to live in the home of his wife, then the wedding takes place at the house of his parents.

20

Livelihood Strategy: Shifting Cultivation

Shifting cultivation is an agricultural system in which plots of land are cultivated temporarily, and then abandoned. In shifting agriculture a plot of land is cleared and cultivated for a short period of time; then it is abandoned and allowed to revert to its natural vegetation while the cultivator moves on to another plot. The period of cultivation is usually terminated when the soil shows signs of infertility or, more commonly, when the field is overrun by weeds. The length of time that a field is cultivated is usually shorter than the period over which the land is allowed to regenerate by fallowing the land. For the natives of Sarawak, paddy planting on a new plot of land is done on an annual basis. This means that they will shift from one plot to another every year, very much on a rotation basis of between three to seven years, depending on the availability of land.

Paddy farming: Land clearing is a vital part of shifting cultivation

Generally, the Kayans of Apoh are farmers. A major part of their livelihood is subsistence paddy farming. Their livelihood evolved around shifting cultivation and hunting. Therefore, this reflects on the fact that the needs of the people are very basic and simple. After all, the daily needs of the people can be easily obtained from the forest and rivers that forms and provides all the livelihood necessities of the community.

Slash and burn method: Hill paddy farming

Slash and burn method is part of hill paddy farming

Traditionally, Kayan agriculture was based on Shifting or swidden paddy cultivation. Agricultural Land in this sense was used and defined primarily in terms of hill paddy farming, fruit gardens, and the forest where they hunt for wild animals and other produce. The Kayans organized their labour in terms of traditionally based land holding groups which determined who owned rights to land and how it is to be used. The "green revolution" in the 1950s, spurred on the planting of new varieties of wetland rice amongst Orang Ulu ethnic groups.

The dependence on subsistence and small-scale agriculture by the Kayans as their main livelihood has made the people active in this occupation. The modern day farming in large scale mono-crop plantations such as palm oil and rubber has affected vast swathes of native land held under customary rights, titles and claims in Sarawak, threaten the local political landscape in various areas in the State. Further problems continue to arise in part due to the shaping of the modern Malaysian nation-states on post-colonial political systems and laws on land tenure. The conflict between the State and the natives on land laws and native customary rights will continue as long as the existing model on land tenure is used against local customary law.

The main precept of land use, in Native Customary Rights (NCR) and under the Brooke and colonial rule, is that cultivated land is owned and held in right by the native owners, and the concept of land ownership was central to this belief. This understanding of *adat* or under the context of NCR is based on the idea that land is used and held under native domain. However, in reality NCR is not binding on the Land Authority of the State, as the natives do not have any legal or document of title to the land. The changes and amendments to the existing Land Code have more or less extinguished the validity of native customary rights to their land. The right to NCR land ownership has to be proven to justify ownership. And how do the natives prove this? Thus, the benefit of the doubt lies very heavily against the native or indigenous people in NCR land ownership.

Paddy planting: The men make holes with sharpened stakes while
the women follow behind and plant the seeds

Work is done on the basis of labour for labour or 'pala-dau'
on a rotation basis for the members that form the group

The growing of hill paddy is linked to the felling of trees of the forest that is often seen as the cause of deforestation. In reality, the situation is grossly exaggerated and not as simple as that. Under shifting cultivation, the natives generally prefer to grow paddy on land which has been used previously that has become a secondary forest for the reason that the trees are small and relatively easy to fell. Studies have suggested that soils under secondary forests are more suitable for paddy planting than soils under old growth forest (Payne, et al 2000).

Traditional shifting paddy cultivation is usually preferred on the fertile alluvial terraces along rivers and the lower slopes of hills. As far as possible, the infertile higher slopes and ridge tops are left under the original primary forest. As such the usual traditional shifting cultivation cannot be seen as the significant cause of loss of primary forests.

There is indeed evidence to show that shifting cultivation amongst the natives of Sarawak has its place in the culture of the people. This has contributed much to the dynamics of sustainable forest ecosystems. The indigenous practice of shifting cultivation of the Kayans allows small plants and animal species which are not adapted to the conditions of primary forests to thrive. Such plants are often favoured foods of larger animals desired for meat. The people also plant various wild fruit trees that boost the natural populations of these valuable plants and providing future food supplies for the wildlife.

Paddy planting 'nugan' practiced by the indigenous tribes of Sarawak

Paddy farming by means of shifting cultivation is normally done on a very small scale - under the concept of subsistence farming. Looking at the practice of shifting cultivation, each family farmed between three to five acres of land each year. This means that the several plots of land of each family is rotated for use after three to seven years which is sufficient time for the land to regain its natural fertility for the next farming season. As already mentioned, shifting cultivation is strictly on the basis of subsistence farming. As such, shifting paddy farming does not have any long term negative impact on the environment.

A Kayan Hill Paddy Farm

The work of paddy planting is divided between the men and women. Men clear the jungle and prepare the ground. In planting the paddy grain, the men walk along and by means of a long pointed stick make holes about one foot apart to contain or receive the seed. The women follow and drop a few grains of paddy into each hole. It was traditionally believed that the latter must be done by women to ensure a more prolific harvest. The feminine touch is presumed to create fructifying potency to the grain the woman touches (Krohn, 1927; 2001). The weeding, after the paddy begins to grow is done by the women of the longhouse in small groups on rotational basis. The women will take turn to weed each other's farm under the context of labour for labour concept or '*pala-dau*'. When the grain has ripened, both men and women do the harvesting.

Kayan Paddy Barn or 'Lepau Parai'

In harvesting, the Kayans cut off the heads of the paddy grains with a little crude tin-knife fixed on a short small bamboo, one stalk at a time, depositing these grain-filled heads into baskets or '*Ingen*' hung from their shoulders or on their back. The harvested grains are kept temporarily in the farm hut if the farm is very far from the longhouse. These will be carried or transported back to the longhouse after the harvest is completed. The paddy grains are gathered up and stored in the family paddy barn or '*lepau parai*' in large baskets or bins made of tree bark. In the old days, when the husk of the paddy grains are needed to be removed to obtain rice or '*bahah*', the women folks will tread or '*mahik*' the paddy stalks to separate the grains which are then dried and pounded towards the evening to complete the arduous and labourious task as there is no rice-mill then. The women pounded the dried paddy in wooden mortars, with pestles or '*alo*" five feet long. As a rule, one or two women use their pestles at one mortar, which is cut out of the trunk of a tree. In this way, the grain is freed from the husk, and is made ready for cooking.

Each family farms its own piece of land. Much of such work as cutting down the jungle and planting is done by a combination of labour or 'pala-dau', several families agreeing to work for each other in turn. By this means all the planting on the land belonging to a particular family is done in one day, and all the grain ripens at the same time.

The practice of shifting cultivation amongst the Kayans of Apoh is very much on the decline though. The people are now turning to long term cash-crop farming and performing work on the basis of paid-labour. Shifting paddy cultivation is no longer a mandatory livelihood strategy in the villages. Thus, shifting paddy cultivation will be an extinct livelihood practice amongst the Kayans in Apoh or the Orang-Ulu communities generally in the future.

Paddy planting activities: Packing the cooked rice. Rice grain pouch and counting the participants are some of the indigenous ways of paddy planting or '*nugan*'.

21

Conservation and preservation of the environment

Enger and Smith (2010) pointed that, the environment is everything that affects an organism during its lifetime, and in turn, all organisms including people affect many components in their environment or ecosystems. An ecosystem is a region in which the organisms and the physical environment form an interacting unit. This is due to the interrelatedness of the components in the environment or ecosystems. For example, the weather affects plants, plants use minerals in the soil and are food for animals, animals spread plant seeds, plants secure the soil, and plants evaporate water, which affects weather. Thus it is very important to manage the environment to sustain its natural biodiversity.

The natural environment around Long Atip village offers numerous and various beautiful landscapes and attractions to nature lovers. One of these natural attractions is an inland lake called *Kaka'*. A trip to *Kaka'* Lake, will take about 10-minute drive from the village. To make a trip to the lake is a worthwhile adventure.

On 22nd December 2005, the launching of the preservation and conservation of the lake was organized by the people of Long Atip. In conjunction with the occasion, a picnic was organized for the whole village to the lake. The lake covers an area of about 100 hectares of water surface that is ideal for water sports and recreation. To add prestige and significance to the event, the Council Negeri representative for Telang Usan, *the Honourable Lihan Jok,* was the guest of honour to officiate the function. Tree planting and the release of about 10,000 fish fries into the lake was officiated by YB *Lihan Jok* as a symbolic gesture to mark the occasion. It is important that some form of conservation of the flora and fauna be done to sustain the various species of indigenous plants, animals and fish of the forest. The 'Tagang System' is a good indigenous way of preserving the fish of the rivers which has been very successful in many parts of Sarawak and Sabah.

The occasion was indeed a time of fun and enjoyment to all the people. Almost all who were present in the longhouse on that day turned up for the picnic.

The flora in the forest around *Kaka'* Lake were diverse and full of exotic wild plants. Effort should be made to preserve and conserve the area to protect the plants, trees and wild animals. The lake can be beautified and maintained as an eco-tourism spot.

The flora and fauna of the native forests is fast depleting though due to over exploitation, commercialization and degradation of the rivers. The prized fish like the *ikan semah* is already very scarce in the Apoh and Melana rivers. Melana River was once teaming with the '*Palau*' fish in the 1970s. Now, one can hardly see this species of fish anymore. Even the wild boars are also very scarce in the jungles. From one informal conversation with Ketua kampong Deng Anyie Long Bemang, he lamented that wild boars are hardly to be hunted anymore and opined that one day the government will have to release young wild-piglets into the wild as what is often done for fish.

Kaka' Inland Lake is just about 10-minute drive from Long Atip.

The jungle around *Kaka'* Lake is rich in flora.

Belian trees are found growing around *Kaka'* Lake

Shorea or *ramin* are found growing around *Kaka'* Lake

'Belaban' or red wood tree is indigenous to the forest of *Kaka'* lake.

Kaka' Lake can be turned into a leisure and eco-tourism park

A day of celebration and picnic at *Kaka'* Lake

The Kayan traditional dress is synonymous to any celebration

The unique attires are well cherished

YB Lihan Jok took time to officiate the *Kaka'* picnic celebration

YB *Lihan Jok* being accorded the honour as the distinguished guest

Puan Freda Mujan Jok the wife of YB *Lihan Jok*

YB *Lihan Jok* was accorded the '*Nyivan joh*' as part of the
welcoming tradition of the Kayan community

YB *Lihan Jok* expressing his closeness and appreciation for the welcome accorded to him by the young dancers

Appreciation souvenir to YB *Lihan Jok*

Celebration Chairman *Nawan Luhat* extending a souvenir to
Puan Freda Mujan Jok the wife of YB *Lihan Jok*

Honourable guests to the *Kaka'* Lake picnic celebration

The Celebration Chairman *Nawan Luhat* giving his welcome address

Ketua Kampong *Amei Kalang Anyie* giving his address

YB *Lihan Jok* giving and officiating the *Kaka'* Lake picnic celebration

A full turnout showed a united community

Ezra and *Alexander* have had an excellent time

A time to cherish and to remember

YB *Lihan Jok* planting a tree to commemorate the occasion

YB *Lihan Jok* about to plant a tree as part of nature conservation

A section of the crowd to the *Kaka'* Lake picnic celebration

Photo call with *Puan Freda Mujan Jok* as remembrance

YB *Lihan Jok* throwing his fishing line for symbolic fishing as a leisure activity

YB *Lihan Jok* releasing fish fries into *Kaka'* Lake

The women of Long Atip provide a strong community spirit

The vicinity of *Kaka'* Lake have a beautiful surrounding and forest

These groups were hard at work barbequing chicken wings

Putting meat into bamboo to make *laho'* or cooking in bamboo

Preparing meat for the *laho'* cooking

Barbequing chicken wings at the Kaka' Lake picnic

The chicken wings were well taken care by everyone

Making sure the chicken wings were well cooked

BBQ chicken wings ready for the picnickers to savour

Everyone were busy giving a helping hand

Alexander was fast learning the BBQ trade

Laho' or cooking in bamboo is one of the traditional ways in Kayan cooking

The conservation and preservation the country's biological diversity is the responsibility of all citizens. The government aspires to conserve its rich biological diversity to ensure that its components are utilized in a sustainable manner for the continued progress and socio-economic development of the nation. Conservation and sustainable utilization of the country's biological diversity centres on the principles (Ministry of Science, Technology and the Environment, 1998) as follows:

- The conservation ethic, including the inherent right to existence of all living forms, is deeply rooted in the belief and cultural values of the people.

- Biological diversity is a national heritage and it must be sustainably managed and wisely utilized today and conserved for future generations.

- Biological resources are natural capital and their conservation is an investment that will yield benefits locally, nationally and globally for the present and future.

- The benefits from sustainable management of biological diversity will accrue directly or indirectly to every sector of society.

- The sustainable management of biological diversity is the responsibility of all sectors of society.

Thus, a natural asset of the country is its wealth in biological diversity. Reduction in this biological diversity will upset the balance within the ecosystem and it is generally accepted that a certain amount of species and genetic diversity is needed to uphold the cyclical relations within the ecosystems and hence maintain ecological functions. Losing diversity means losing the ecosystem reliance, leading to adverse effects on human lives. Loss of genetic resources, floods, deterioration in quantity and quality of water supply, decline in food supply, loss in productive soils, and loss in potentially useful biological resources are some of the detrimental effe ts of the reduction in or loss of biological diversity.

According to the Ministry of Science, Technology and the Environment, (1998), the country is rich in plant genetic resources. For example, fruit resources are very diverse. There are 28 species of durian (*Durio*) and its relatives in the country. All with the exception of *D. Zibethinus* are wild. The mangoes are equally rich with 22 species, but only three or four species of these are being utilized.

There are 49 species of *mangosteen* but only *Garcinia mangostana* is popularly eaten. Other examples of large genera with edible fruits include *Artocarpus* (cempedak) and *Nephelium* (rambutan).

As for animal genetic resources, they relate to livestock or farm animals. Our jungle fowls, wild pigs, buffaloes, cattle and local goats are considered true indigenous species. Non-indigenous animals are mainly breeding chickens, pigs, cattle and goats which have been imported into the country from all over the world. Importation of these animals has enriched the gene pool of the different species considerably.

The rich biological resources have given rise to a rich cultural heritage of sustainable use amongst the indigenous people of the country, especially those dependent on the forest for their livelihood. The elements of the rich cultural heritage that relate to nature are reflected in handicrafts, the beliefs and traditional system and the use of plants and animals of the forest. The indigenous tribes of Sarawak, for instance, have used the sago of a palm (Eugeissona utilis) that is found in the wild of the forest (Ministry of Science, Technology and the Environment, 1998). The need to enforce the practice of conservation like the indigenous '*Tagang System*' and the creation of more conservation parks should be strongly advocated by all stakeholders.

22

Challenges into the future

The Kayans of Apoh River has come a long way to revive and rekindle the dances, songs, music and merriments that form the core elements of the rich Kayan cultural heritage. The Kayans of Long Bemang have organized a *Sape* Music Festival in 1999, numerous Music workshops in Long Bedian and the yearly home-coming celebrations in Long Atip. The rich cultural melting pot of the Kayan Uma Pu can be found in the Apoh River valley. The strength, cooperation and altruistic values of *Kayan Uma Pu* lies in the protection and preservation of their culture and upholding their class structure of *Maren Uma* as the dominant leadership inheritance of the tribe. The challenges and significance of preserving and sustaining these cultures is the common goal of the *Kayan Uma Pu*, for the sake of the future generations.

The village of Long Atip for instance, is indeed filled with treasure troves of rich Kayan traditional cultures and unique ways of life. Home is always the best of all places. And the reality is that, people will continue to seek their roots. There will be many more generations of our children and grandchildren to come though, whereby they will definitely seek their roots. The instinct and desire to return to their roots will naturally evolve through the generations. Thus, the present generation of *Kayan Uma Pu* has a noble duty to preserve their homeland for the sake of the future generations.

Therefore, for the sake of our future grandchildren, we must continue to maintain our Kayan *Uma Pu* root in the Apoh River Valley. For the sons and daughters of Apoh River Valley, no place is better than home. The sound of the *Sape* and the drumming of the *tawaks* are all clear signals of the revival and renaissance of the rich Kayan cultures of the Apoh River valley of the past, present and reverberating alive into the future generations of the Kayan tribe.

The cultures and way of life of the indigenous people especially the *Kayan Uma Pu* are indeed blessed with the beauty of nature which is rich in biodiversity that should be managed in a sustainable manner for the sake of the future. The sustainable management of biological diversity is indeed the responsibility of all sectors of society.

As such, how do we need to harness the Kayan Uma Pu for their resilience, competitiveness and competitive edge as they move into the future? The highly protective environment that we have in the country is a factor that we are facing and confronting in almost all spheres of endeavours and vocation. The challenges against the Orang Ulu and more so the Kayan Uma Pu is so real, obvious and insidious. The Orang Ulu or the 'interior people' are seen as backward, ignorant and 'jungle people', tags that are belittling the community. In terms of numbers, they are seen as 'weak voice', insignificant, and of no obvious impact to any authority and decisions. As such, there is no real and expected threat from the community. Therefore, the questions of how these kinds of perceptions, ideas and thinking came about? And how do the 'Maren Uma', community leaders and the people's representatives' guide and steer the community forward?

Therefore, it is long overdue for the community to reassess, analyze and re-invent their future. They need to be a major player for decision-making process that determine and chart the future progress and development of the country. Being a minority, they need to position themselves to be the 'King Maker', the crucial factor in critical and important decisions.

The Orang Ulu should pursue and strive for dignity and respect that is rightly theirs like those earlier times of Temenggong Oyong Lawai Jau, and Penghulu Tama Paya Anyie Usung. Nonetheless, they need to build and strengthen the very core of their foundation as a group, race and tribe. The community need to pursue passionately the spirit of bonding and kinsmanship of the Hipun Uma, Maren Uma and the community specifically. Indeed the community is at the cross-road of defining their future as '*Orang Ulu*'. Realistically, there are no more places in the country that is considered as '*Ulu*' or interior due to the advent of progress and development, and especially in the context of lateral thinking (de Bono, 1967). Those 'hidden hands' (Todaro, 1994)) will always want to keep the community poor, dependent and subordinated to those in power and majority so as to maintain the status quo.

We need to develop strategies to propel the community to be dynamic and progressive to move in tandem with Vision 2020 (Ahmad Sarji, 1993). We want our Orang Ulu Community to get the share of the development cake as envisioned by the government. Perhaps we may take a cue from an indigenous community that has come up with seven prong strategies Satu (1997) as follows:

❖ To be a highly dynamic, well educated and informed community towards the acquisition and adoption of excellence in scientific, technological and ICT knowledge that promotes advancement in literacy and academic excellence in the community.

- ❖ Building a resilient, proactive, competitive, self-sustaining and synergistic community.

- ❖ Raising the economic, social and physical infrastructures towards the betterment of the livelihood of the community.

- ❖ Preserving and promoting the historical and cultural heritage of the community.

- ❖ Conservation and sustainable land use, and the alienation, demarcation and codification of NCR lands for the benefit and betterment of the individual landowners and community.

- ❖ No family in the community is to live below the poverty line by the year 2015.

- ❖ Development of integrated agro-eco tourism industry as an engine of economic growth and opportunity towards an integral and overall betterment of the community.

The young generation of Orang Ulu or *Kayan Uma Pu* specifically are highly capable and well-educated who are eager to accept the challenges of responsible management and authority. We must give them an active role in modern governance and business charging them with real responsibility and showing them respect and trust. By redefining and imposing responsibility in this way, the Orang Ulu will maximize their 'moment of truth' (Carlzon, 1987). They will facilitate the transformation of the Orang Ulu and, thereby secure an important competitive advantage.

References

Ahmad Sarji, A.H. (1993). *Malaysia's Vision 2020. Understanding the Concept, Implications and Challenges.* Petaling Jaya: Pelanduk Publications.

Armstrong, M. (1995). *Personnel management practice.* (Fifth Edition). London: Kogan Page.

Axelrod, R. (1984). *The Evolution of cooperation.* New York: Basic Books Inc. Publishers.

Bibi Aminah, A.G., Dit, T.J., Venkatasawmy, R. (2009). *Sarawak Culture: Pelah Hawa Traditional Kayan Wedding.* Kuching: Pustaka Negeri Sarawak. http://www.pustaka-sarawak.com/Pustaka-Sarawak/Sarawakiana/ pelahhawa/after_wedding.html Available on-line on 25.1.2013

Blaug, M. (1972). *Introduction to the Economics of Education.* London: Harmondsworth.

Bloom, D.A, Engelhart, M. D, Furst, E.J, Hill, W.H, & Krathwohi, D.R. (1956). *Taxonomy of educational objectives: the classification of educational goals; Handbook 1: Cognitive Domain.* New York: Longmans.

Bloom, B.S. (1956) p. 4 "The idea for this classification system was formed at an informal meeting of college examiners attending the 1948 *American Psychological Association* Convention in Boston.

Bloom, B. S. (1994). *Reflections on the development and use of the taxonomy* in Anderson, Lorin W. & Lauren A. Sosniak, (Eds.), *Bloom's Taxonomy: A Forty-Year Retrospective.* Chicago National Society for the Study of Education

Borneo Post (May 9, 2002). *Long Bedian is best village*. Miri: *The Borneo Post.*

Carlzon, J. (1987). *Moments of Truth*. New York: Harper & Row Publishers.

Daft, R. (2000). *Management*. (Fifth Edition). Orlando: Harcourt College Publishers.

De Bono, E. (1967). *The use of Lateral Thinking*. London: Penguin Books

Enger E.D. & Smith, B.F. (2010). *Environmental Science: A study of interrelationships*. (12th Edition). New York: McGraw-Hill

Feldman, H. (1959). *"The Problem of Personal Names as a Universal Element in Culture." American Imago* 16, P: 237-250.

Florides, A. (2003). Human Capital: A Theoretical Outline. Available on line. http://www.maths. tcd.ie/local/JUNK/econrev/ser/html/hkap2.html. Retrieved on 9. 6. 2003.

Fong, H.K. (2008). *A History of the Development of Baram River Basin in Sarawak*. Kuching: The Sarawak Press.

Gomes, E.H. (1911). *Seventeen years among the Sea Dyaks of Borneo*. Kota Kinabalu: Natural History Publications.

Hardin, G. (1968). *The tragedy of the commons*. Available on-line on 5.12.2003. *http://dieoff.com/ page95.htm*

Hellwig, M.F. (2003). *Public good provision with many participants*. Review of Economic Studies 70: 589 - 614.

Hogg, M.A. (1992). *The social psychology of group cohesiveness*. London: Harvester Wheatsheaf.

Hose, C. & McDougall, W. (1912). *The Pagan Tribes of Borneo. A description of their physical moral and intellectual condition with some discussion of their ethnic relations*. London Macmillan and Co. http://archive.org/stream/pagantribesofbor02hoseuoft/pagantribesofbor02hoseuoft_djvu. txt. Available on-line on 31.7.2013

Hose, C. (1926) (1988). *Natural Man. A record from Borneo.* Singapore: Oxford University Press.

Krohn, W.O. (1927: 2001). *In Borneo Jungles among the Dayak* Headhunters. Shah Alam: Oxford University Press.

McConnell, C. & Brue, S. (1989). Contemporary Labour Economics. New York: McGraw-Hill.

Ministry of Science, Technology and the Environment. (1998*). National Policy on Biological Diversity.* Kuala Lumpur: Institut Terjemahan Negara Malaysia Berhad.

Najib Tun Razak (1995). Human Capital – the Key to Malaysia's Success. Welcome address during a seminar entitled "Malaysia's Human Capital Requirement: Challenges Ahead" organized by Malaysian Strategic Research Centre on 11 April 1995. Available on line. *http://www.jobstreet. com.my/employers/hrm3.htm.* Retrieved on 8. 7. 2003.

Neubeck, K.J. & Glasberg, D.S. (2005). *Sociology, Diversity, Conflict, and Change.* New York: McGraw-Hill.

Payne, J., Cubitt, G, Lau, D. And Langub, J. (2000). *This is Borneo.* London: New Holland Publishers (UK) Ltd.

Roth, H.L. (1968). *The Natives of Sarawak and British North Borneo Volume I.* Kuala Lumpur: University of Malaya Press.

Santrock, J.W. (2011). *Educational Psychology.* (5th Edition). New York: McGraw Hill International.

Satu, S. A. (1997). *Mission statement for the development of the Lun Bawang community Sarawak.* Lawas: Lun Bawang Association.

Scriven, M. & Paul, R. (1987). *Critical Thinking and Education Reform.* Presented at the 8th Annual International Conference on Critical Thinking and Education Reform, Summer 1987.

Smith, E. C. (1967). *Treasury of Name Lore.* New York: Harper & Row.

Southwell, C.H. (1999). *Uncharted Waters.* Calgary: Astana Publishing

Spencer, E. S. (2003). *Ingredients of Economic Growth*. Lecture notes to SLUSE students. Kuching: UNIMAS

State Planning Unit. (2011). *Sarawak: Facts and Figures 2011*. Kuching: Chief Minister's Department.

Steinbach, R. L. (1993). *The Adult Learner: Strategies for Success*. Menlo Park, CA: Crisp Publications.

Stoner, J.A.F., Freeman, R.E., & Gilbert Jr., D.R. (1995). *Management*. (Sixth Edition). Englewood Cliffs: Prentice-Hall International.

Todaro, M.P. (1994). *Economic Development*. (Sixth Edition). New York: Longman.

Triandis, H.C. (1994). Culture and Social Behaviour. In Lonner, W.J. & Malpass, R.S. (Editors) of *Psychology and Culture*. Boston: Allyn and Bacon.

Tuomela, R. (2000). Cooperation – A philosophical study. Available on-line on 24. 10. 2003. *http://www.valt.helsinki.fi/staff/tuomela/papers/cont.html*.

Wikipedia. *Dayak People*. http://en.wikipedia.org/wiki/Dayak_people Available on-line on 25.01.2013

Woolfolk, A. (2010). *Education Psychology*. (11th Edition). Upper Saddle River: Pearson Education International.

World Bank (2003). Education and the World Bank. Available on line. *http://www1.worldbank.org/education/pdf/opendoors.pdf*. Retrieved on 4. 7. 2003.